The Tarpon Club of Texas

And the Genius of E.H.R. Green

R.K. Sawyer & Jim Moloney

The Tarpon Club of Texas

And the Genius of E.H.R. Green

R.K. Sawyer & Jim Moloney

www.nuecespress.com
Corpus Christi, Texas

The Tarpon Club of Texas is dedicated to
our loving and patient wives, Wendy and Candace.

Library of Congress Control Number: 2022914450

Sawyer, R. K and Jim Moloney

The Tarpon Club of Texas, The Genius of E.H.R. Green

Includes index.

1. E.H.R. Green
2. Hetty Green
3. Port Aransas — History.
4. St. Joseph Island
5. Sport Fishing History
6. Waterfowl Hunting History
7. Yacht Racing History
8. The Aransas Pass channel
9. Coastal Bend of Texas

ISBN   978-1-7339524-5-3

Published by Nueces Press, Corpus Christi, Texas.

Cover design by Jeff Chilcoat

www.nuecespress.com

TABLE OF CONTENTS

PUBLISHER'S NOTE

Years ago, I purchased some photographs of the Tarpon Club on the internet. Later, I purchased an 1899 membership booklet of the Tarpon Club on ebay.™ At the time I knew nothing about this forgotten piece of Texas history. Over the years I found more information and began to discover some of the fascinating history behind the short-lived club. My good friend Murphy Givens wrote one of his weekly history columns in the *Corpus Christi Caller Times* on the club.

When Rob Sawyer wrote his three books on the history of duck and goose hunting in Texas, he included some of my photos of the club in his books. I was surprised at Rob's ability to ferret out information from long-ignored sources to compile his works.

One weekend morning in the fall of 2020, after Rob's third book was published, I was perusing his work. He wrote that it would be his last book. That inspired me to reach out to Rob about collaboration on yet another book – this one. We are fortunate that he took up my challenge.

I am amazed at Rob's ability to find references to the Tarpon Club, tarpon fishing, duck hunting, yachting, E.H.R. Green and various club members in 130-year-old publications. He has discovered the history of the creation of the Tarpon Club and its short life as the exclusive fishing and hunting club of rich and successful men at the turn of the last century.

Another enlightenment was the life of E.H.R. "Ned" Green, the son and heir to Hetty Green—the "witch" of Wall Street and the richest woman in the United States, famed as an eccentric miser. Ned founded and controlled the Tarpon Club and invited the cream of American business and politics to join him in the pursuit of fish and fowl for his political aims.

Jim Moloney
Nueces Press

FOREWORD

I was supposed to be retired. At least until Jim Moloney called, curious if I was interested in researching E.H.R. "Ned" Green with him. Jim and I worked together on Green's Tarpon Club for an earlier project, and he thought the topic and the man justified a more complete study. The combination of Jim Moloney and E.H.R. Green was a powerful pull.

The subject of Ned Green, I learned, defied expectations. Before this project, my knowledge was confined to just one of his achievements, the Tarpon Club. During its brief life, it was the greatest sporting club in America. That topic alone would have filled the pages of a book. But two years into the current research, my jumble of notes revealed that Ned Green was a far more complex and accomplished figure than I imagined, and it confirmed Jim's suspicions.

I used to hunt ducks, mostly redheads, on shorelines that were once part of the Tarpon Club haunts. During this project, I learned that my great-great grandfather, J.B.C. Lucas, was a founding Tarpon Club member. I suspect I retraced the steps of my great-great grandfather. I'll never know.

Some people paint, their compiled brushstrokes an artform. Others compose or perform music. I can do neither. One day I crafted a sentence, bursting with adjectives, color, and meaning. To me, it was art. When that sentence was combined with thousands of others, the outcome was my first natural history book. And it was terrible. Wisely, I edited each chapter over a hundred times before publication and in the end, the sentences were less offensive. Four books and uncountable articles later, the writing got easier, improved, and in places might even be considered good. My hope is that you, the reader, will find that at least some of the sentences that make up the E.H.R. Green story are good.

ACKNOWLEDGEMENTS

The authors are indebted to Mary Jo O'Rear, Cliff Strain, and Mark Creighton and the Port Aransas Preservation and Historical Association, and the staff at the Corpus Christi Public Library for material covering parts of E.H.R. and Mabel Green's Texas years. Justin Parkoff and Sam Watson of the Texas Maritime Museum graciously rummaged through the attic of the Maritime Museum in Rockport in search of yachting images on our behalf.

The authors are also deeply appreciative for assistance provided by fishing historian Ed Pritchard, who made his meticulous research available to us and allowed the use of period tarpon reel images.

We, like every modern Texas researcher, benefited from the material digitized as part of the Portal to Texas History. It has allowed us to build stories from references never easily available in the past.

A special thank you goes to Bob Geary, whose Round Hill recollections helped bring that important subject to life.

Images from the Green's Massachusetts years were graciously provided by Bob Collum, who assisted us with photographs from the Leslie Jones Collection archived in the Boston Public Library, Sarah Hagon of the Boston Public Library, Mark Procknik and Cecelia Tavares of the New Bedford Whaling Museum, Jodi Goodman of the New Bedford Free Public Library, Caroline White from the University of Massachusetts Amherst Libraries, the Library of Congress, Dixon Gutierrez at the State Library and Archives of Florida.

Finally, we are indebted to David Sikes, our thorough and enthusiastic manuscript editor, who was responsible for introducing the two of us so many years ago.

PROLOGUE

America at the end of the 19th century was basking in industrial and financial prosperity. Those were heady times for men in professions such as law, medicine, and politics, but particularly for finance and business. It was the era of unregulated banking and investing, and they were making up the rules as they went. The most successful players possessed not just ambition, intellect, and courage but usually cunning, greed, and ruthlessness.

Some from the halls of power were outdoorsmen. Many were gentleman sportsmen and conservationists, while others conveyed the same approach to sporting activities that they did to business. For them, time afield was less about leisure than a competition to bag the largest volume, rarest, biggest, or most dangerous game fish or animal. Part of the attraction was the challenge and thrill of the chase. Part of it was that – much like a financial statement – what they killed or caught was measurable.

American leisure was made possible not just from financial resources, but from advancements in technology. Railroad tracks now crisscrossed the continent, allowing for travel to formerly remote parts of the countryside via comfortable dining and sleeping cars. Steam was replacing sails on America's waterways, and gasoline engines would make their appearance by the end of the century. Improvements in the outdoorsmen's tools also played a role, notably in firearms and fishing tackle that made it possible to kill or catch larger numbers and bigger trophies.

One of the most recognized names in the gilded sporting world at the turn of the century was E.H.R. "Ned" Green, an accomplished railroad man, banker, politician, and founder of the nation's most extravagant sporting club – The Tarpon Club – before he was 30 years old. Ned was the one-legged son of Hetty Howland Robinson Green, the richest woman in the world. America was fascinated with the eccentricities and parsimony of Hetty Green, a financial genius, who triumphed during an era when women ordinarily did not rule business empires.

When Hetty Green's son opened the Tarpon Club in 1899 it was the most expensive, expansive, and exclusive club in the world. Green selected the location for his club on the sand flats of St. Joseph Island, a barrier island at the edge of the Gulf of Mexico, adjacent to the Aransas Pass, in the Coastal Bend of Texas. It was one of the nation's last remaining strongholds for huge numbers of wintering waterfowl, and the remainder of the year it was rivaled by only Florida as the country's most prolific tarpon and big-game fishing destination.

The two-story clubhouse that rose from the sand was constructed of cypress and pine, and encompassed over 12,000 square feet, its exterior colors a contrast of gleaming white against bold green window trimmings and a red-shingled roof. The first floor housed private offices, billiard rooms, kitchen, dining rooms, and a dance hall, with a large open veranda. On the second floor were 18 sleeping rooms, servant quarters, and a parlor "fitted up with an especial view of making ladies comfortable." Copper screens covered each door and window. An electrical plant that powered 126 "incandescent lamps" provided a "bewildering and beautiful" spectacle that could be seen for miles.

Tarpon Club members reached the town of Rockport, the closest town on the mainland to St. Joseph Island, via the San Antonio & Aransas Pass Railroad. Port town politicos predicted that "hundreds of influential and wealthy sportsmen will flock to our Texas fishing and hunting resort," and anxiously anticipated the "steam yachts of Eastern millionaires." From the Rockport wharves, club members and guests crossed eight miles of Aransas Bay to the Tarpon Club in schooners or Green's personal yacht the *Mabel*. Named for Green's paramour, former prostitute Mabel Harlow, the cruiser was better known as the first gasoline launch in Texas.

Green's sporting venture opened in 1899, and in its first year dubbed its membership the "First Four Hundred Sportsmen of

America," a privileged group with "more politicians and businessmen that in any other similar organization in the United States" and whose "wealth combined reaches into the hundred-millions." Under the headline "Playground of the first 400 Sportsmen of America," several newspapers announced an unparalleled membership roster that included President William McKinley and former president Grover Cleveland. Neither were club members. No matter that it wasn't true. E.H.R. Green savored the attention and turn-of-the-century America was infatuated with everything Tarpon Club.

The hyperbole that was the Tarpon Club faded quickly. Press coverage began to go silent within just three years of its 1899 opening ceremony. By 1904, the club was closed. The reason it ended prematurely is as esoteric as Green's motivation for opening it in the first place.

Tarpon Club founder E.H.R. Green was a gifted man, and the Tarpon Club, despite its over-sized reputation, was not his greatest achievement. It's hard to determine what was – the list includes his role as president of the Texas Midland Railroad, runs at the Texas governor's seat, a litany of inventions and patents, groundbreaking agricultural and horticulture practices, popularizing early automobile racing, navigating his mother's financial empire, and assembling one of the nation's greatest collections of rare books, coins, stamps – and pornography.

Tarpon Club founder E.H.R. Green was also a flawed man, with enormous cravings and appetites. Everything he touched had to be bigger, better, more opulent, or more expensive than anyone who came before him. One of his passions was sex, and his inability to control its urges was perhaps one of the main reasons he never achieved the political prominence he so desperately sought.

The many facets of E.H.R. Green make his story unique. Yet at its core, it is also a story repeated throughout the annals of American history. The only things that need to change are the place, the backdrop, and the times. But because this story is about E.H.R. Green, he'd assume that it would have to be bigger, and better, than any that came before or after.

E.H.R. Green's Tarpon Club

CHAPTER 1

BEGINNINGS

It was a singular place, a confluence of diverse waterways and landforms colliding over a small geographic area in an expanse of the Texas coast known as Coastal Bend. To the east, the Gulf of Mexico converged at the shoreline of the barrier islands of St. Joseph and Mustang islands, their shifting, shimmering dunes sprinkled with drift and timbers amidst a covering of sea oats and seacoast bluestem grasses. A succession of bay brush and *Spartina* grasses, then *Salicornia*, marked where the dunes graded into the tidal flats of the bay shore.

The narrow barrier islands barely rising from the sea were created from sand derived from the continent, transported by rivers, then continuously reworked from offshore bars and wind-driven aeolian clastics of the South Texas sand sheet. Everything about the barrier islands was ephemeral, their ever-changing morphology shaped by counterclockwise littoral currents that eroded sands from the north and redeposited them to the south.

Between the barrier islands and the mainland were the estuaries, elongated in shape, their seagrass flats dissected by shallow bars. To the north was Aransas Bay, punctuated by the northwest-southeast-trending Long Reef and Deadman's Island. Aransas Bay formed a narrow neck as it approached Corpus Christi Bay. Arcuate fingers of water extended down the bayside to Blind Pass and Mud Island, jutting into the bay before Lydia Ann Island and the Lydia Ann Channel adjacent to the Aransas Pass channel. Gulf waters ebbed and flowed by wind-driven tides through the pass, allowing for an exchange between saline Gulf waters and more brackish bay waters.

Located between St. Joseph and Mustang Islands, the pass was subject to the whims of sands that accumulated and aggraded onto the southern tip of St. Joseph Island. The process was so rapid that, in the 30 years between 1857 to 1888, the pass migrated a mile to the south. North winds following winter cold fronts pushed bay water with sufficient energy to scour each new location of the pass, keeping it deep enough to allow passage of 19th-century sailing ships for at least parts of each year.

Aransas Pass was both a blessing and a bane to early mariners. The latter was attested to by the ribs of ship hulls that protruded from the waterline, silent testament to mariners who either stranded in the breakers on the outside bar, or whose soundings overlooked a shifting bar in the inlet. If they made it through the pass, helmsmen still had to reckon with the channel's sharp bends where it met the tidal wash-over delta of Harbor Island.

Harbor Island went by different names – Curlew Island in the 1830s, then Low Island, and after the Civil War, the Big Flats. Situated between the open Gulf and the shallow bays, the skyline above its winding bayous and mangroves was a swirling mass of motion and color from summer rookeries of roseate spoonbills, herons, and pelicans, and in the winter flocks of migratory birds that animated the horizon. Equally as vibrant were its fringing waterways, with surfaces rippling, splashing, and exploding with mullet, seatrout, redfish, dolphins, and the silver king – tarpon.

Aransas Pass and its environs were described by a mariner in 1842 as a "multitude of islands, shoals, flats, false channels, etc., which I undertake to say, would have puzzled a smuggler's pilot." It was a hard place for man to tame. Partly this was due to nature, as harsh as it was bountiful. Partly it was a product of human nature, with its conflicts, politics, ambitions, and avarice. It was a place where, in most instances, dreams and schemes that played out on it shores spanned but a few short years. The Tarpon Club, as extraordinary as it was, would prove to be no different.

The People of the Pass. The first European footprints in coastal Texas were those of the Spaniards during the 16th century, a time when caravels, galleons, and brigantines carried the adventurous to the New World in pursuit of land and riches. Spanish explorer Alonzo Álvarez de Pineda was likely first, including the waterway, later called Corpus Christi Bay, on the map of the Gulf of Mexico he sent to the emperor in 1519.

Governor Pánfilo de Narváez led a second journey, embarking in 1527 with 600 soldiers and settlers. A year into their Florida expedition, Narváez's lieutenant Álvar Núñez Cabeza de Vaca and a greatly diminished number of the original crew would wash ashore on the Gulf Coast. The onerous expedition of de Vaca and a handful of other survivors as they struggled to reach Mexico – lasting some eight years and covering 2,400 miles – provided one of the first written accounts of the Texas coast.

It was 127 years later that Frenchman René Robert Cavelier, Sieur de La Salle attempted to claim this same land for France. LaSalle's colonization struggle was as arduous as de Vaca's before him. Assaults by the native population, disease, hunger, and slayings within the party – including that of La Salle – whittled away at the remaining Frenchmen. Some survivors made their way to French Canada and a few were to remain among the native population.

The first effective settlement on St. Joseph Island, in the late 1810s, was likely a fort manned by privateer Jean Lafitte, its location nearly the same as E.H.R. Green selected for the site of the Tarpon Club almost a century later. After Lafitte abandoned the Gulf Coast and sailed into a fate unknown, some of his crew later returned, establishing a small maritime settlement called Aransas Town (not to be confused with a similarly named town on Live Oak peninsula). Likely they were joined by a few Irish and Mexican colonist families of empresarios James Power and James Hewetson, who settled

3

part of Coastal Bend through a contract with the Mexican government.

Zachary Taylor established a small supply post on St. Joseph Island at the onset of the Mexican American War, landing some 3,500 soldiers on its shores in August 1845. The bulk of the army then moved to Corpus Christi before marching south to the Rio Grande and the battles of Palo Alto and Resaca de la Palma in 1846.

The St. Joseph Island population waxed and waned during the late 1840s to 1860s. At its core were ship captains, bar pilots, and lightermen who guided ships from the Gulf through Aransas Pass or ferried cargo from sea-going ships to shallow-draft lighters. The future of St. Joseph Island seemed bright in the 1850s. Steamships sailed between the pass and New Orleans, the increasing volume of maritime commerce justifying Congress to commission a lighthouse on Harbor Island to mark the entrance to Aransas Bay through the Aransas Pass.

Tennessee railroad promoter Albert Miller Lea, who dreamed of constructing a deepwater port and developing the barrier islands, planned a railroad from San Antonio to the Aransas Pass that would link to a transcontinental route between the Mississippi River and the Pacific coast. The Civil War ended his aspirations. The Civil War also ended Aransas Town, a victim of Union blockades, bombardments by Federal gunships, and landing parties that burned many of its buildings.

Only three years after the War, Rockport investors cast their eye on the future, investing $10,000 to build a 600-foot dike to stabilize Aransas Pass for navigation. Their timber frame jetty, packed with stone and brush, washed away after two years. Aransas Town had something of a rebirth in the 1870s, only to be erased by the great Indianola hurricane of September 1875. The few remaining St. Joseph settlers relocated across the channel to Mustang Island.

The southern tip of St. Joseph Island was largely abandoned by the time the iron-hulled Morgan merchant steamship *Mary* grounded on an outside bar during a heavy swell on November

30, 1876. The Mustang Island Mercer family of bar pilots successfully conveyed each passenger to safety before the ship went to pieces, the vessel and cargo left to salvagers and the sea.

Taming the Pass. The wrecking of the *Mary* hastened the US government to commission a lifesaving station on Mustang Island in 1878, and the next year embarked on a project to deepen Aransas Pass by constructing jetties and revetments. The project was assigned to US Engineer Major Samuel M. Mansfield, who steamed into Rockport in May 1879. Ironically, Mansfield arrived as the body of pioneer Aransas deepwater visionary, Pryor Lea, was headed to Goliad in a "metallic casket" for internment.

Engineer Mansfield's crews set to work in 1880, completing a 4,000-foot jetty south of the pass using brush mattresses overlaid with stone. Called the Mansfield or Old Government Jetty, the project slowed the rate of erosion but did not realize its goal of creating a channel deep enough for ocean-going steamers.

Investment schemes came and went throughout the 1880s and 90s. Promotional pieces promulgating the next big project came from private firms such as the Texas Homestead and Farmers Association, Aransas Pass Land Company, Aransas Pass Harbor Company, Aransas Harbor City and Improvement Company, and Harbor City Company.

At the heart each scheme was always improvement of the pass, involving construction of, or improvement to, the original Mansfield Jetty; the Nelson Jetty on Mustang Island; and the Haupt or North Jetty across the Pass, an innovative attempt to imitate river processes of aggradation and channel erosion but that only succeeded in eliminating the flow of the original, natural scouring process.

It didn't matter if the source for manpower and funding was private or government, efforts to tame the pass were always the same – more furtive jetty concepts and more aborted land development schemes. By the time E.H.R Green and his future Tarpon Club entourage visited the white, hard-packed sand of St. Joseph Island in 1898, no one was living on its southern end.

Across the pass was a small maritime hamlet of fishermen and government jetty workers. Originally named Ropesville for the architect of several failed developments in Corpus Christi and on Mustang Island, it had been rechristened Tarpon. It was staking its future on the hope that a single game fish – the silver king – might reverse its fortunes.

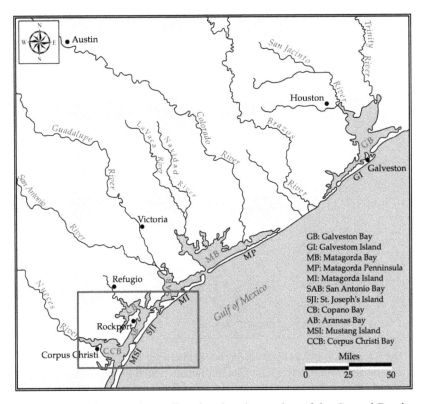

The Texas Gulf Coast, the outline showing the portion of the Coastal Bend frequented by Tarpon Club members and their hunting and fishing guides. Maritime travel or horse and buggy were the only way to reach Coastal Bend before railroad infrastructure reached Rockport in the 1880s. Illustration by R.K. Sawyer.

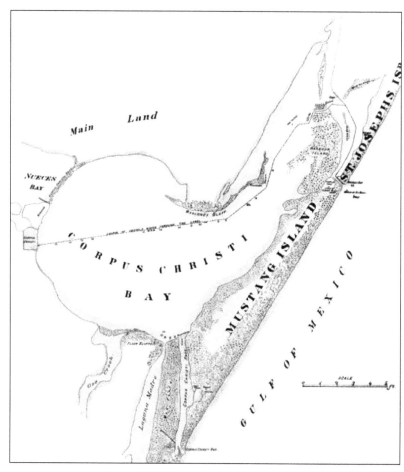

The Tarpon Club was located on the southern tip of St Joseph Island, one mile north of the Aransas Pass Channel across from the lighthouse on Harbor Island. The club was eight miles south of Rockport on the mainland, and situated one mile north of Tarpon, Texas (Port Aransas) at the northern end of Mustang Island. The town of Corpus Christi was some twenty miles to the west as the crow flies, but nearly 30 miles by boat. Boat captains reached Corpus Christi from the Gulf by first negotiating the Aransas Pass channel, then setting a course to the north and around Harbor Island. Although it would have been shorter to sail south of Harbor Island, the shoal waters of Turtle Cove were not navigable. Once Harbor Island was cleared, vessels tacked down its west bank to Corpus Christi Bay. When Richard King and the Corpus Christi Navigation Company dredged the Morris and Cummins Cut in 1874, it provided the first artery for shallow draft sailing vessels to access Corpus Christi. See also map on page 57. Collection of Jim Moloney.

7

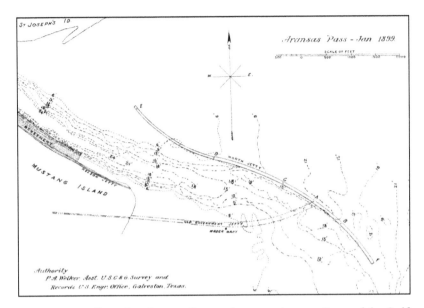

Aransas Pass allowed exchange of waters between Aransas Bay and the Gulf of Mexico. As a result of littoral currents of the Gulf of Mexico and prevailing southeast winds, the pass was constantly shifting and moving south. The shifting channel of Aransas Pass long tested mariners, its challenges giving rise to skilled local seamen known as "bar pilots" who assisted in maneuvering visiting ships safely to and from the Gulf. Shipwrecks were common, particularly for vessels who did not employ bar pilots, which created another thriving maritime industry – opportunities for rescue and salvage operations. This chart by the U. S. Engineers Office in Galveston, Texas is dated January 1899, about the time that the Tarpon Club opened. Collection of Jim Moloney

8

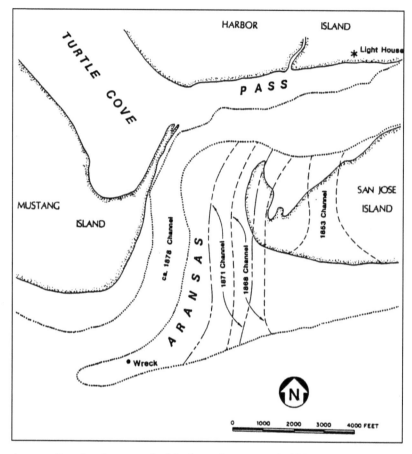

Aransas Pass has been navigable throughout recorded history. Prior to the construction of revetments and jetties, the pass migrated at rates of up to 280 ft. per year. The chart above illustrates the migration of the pass from 1863, when it was approximately opposite the lighthouse, to 1868, 1871 and 1878. During those years the pass moved about one mile. After the successful construction of jetties, the pass was at last stabilized. The wreck shown on the map is the remains of the steamship *Mary*. Image from *Underwater Archaeology of the Wreck of the Steamship Mary (41NU2522) and Assessment of Seven Anomalies, Corpus Christi Entrance Channel, Nueces County, Texas.* Collection of Jim Moloney.

9

This portion of an 1853 U. S. Coast Survey, *Reconnaissance of ARANSAS PASS*, shows the settlement of Aransas approximately two miles north of the Aransas Pass (lower left). It was located at the site of an "old government warehouse" abandoned when the U.S. Army relocated from the Coastal Bend at the commencement of the Mexican American War. Collection of Jim Moloney.

The steamship *Mary* was built in 1866 for the Morgan lines by the Harlan & Hollingsworth Company for Gulf Coast service between cities such as New Orleans, Mobile, and other smaller ports such as Rockport. The ship had an iron hull with a wooden superstructure and was powered by a low-pressure condensing steam engine. The side-wheeler ship could easily reach speeds of 12 miles per hour.

On the morning of November 30, 1876, the *Mary* ran aground on a bar in rough seas while attempting to enter the Aransas Pass without the assistance of local bar pilots. All passengers and crew were rescued from the stranded vessel before she sank. She was carrying a full cargo of assorted merchandise from New Orleans bound for Rockport and Corpus Christi. Some cargo, such as wagon parts and wheels, was later salvaged using grappling hooks but most was never recovered. The *Mary* was insured for $125,000 but there was no estimate placed on the value of the lost cargo.

This wreck was the impetus for the U.S. Government to attempt to tame the pass. A lifesaving station was established, and jetties and revetments were authorized, although the process would take some thirty years. Image is from *Underwater Archaeology of the Wreck of the Steamship Mary (41NU2522) and Assessment of Seven Anomalies, Corpus Christi Entrance Channel, Nueces County, Texas.* Collection of Jim Moloney.

.

CHAPTER 2

BECOMING E.H.R. GREEN

E.H.R. "Ned" Green's father, Edward, was head of an East China trading company in the Philippines and China before returning to the United States and marrying New England blue blood Hetty Robinson in 1867. He made and lost several fortunes to Wall Street speculation, particularly railroads. By the time Ned was building his St. Joseph Island Tarpon Club oasis, his father was living mostly alone in quiet obscurity in his native Vermont. He died there in 1902.

Ned's mother was Hetty Howland Robinson, born in 1834 to a wealthy Quaker family. Hetty's grandfather, Isaac Howland Jr., founded a whaling company in New Bedford, Massachusetts that grew into what was probably the largest maritime operation in America. Edward Mott Robinson, her father, was a partner in the Howland enterprise of New England seamen and ship owners.

Edward M. Robinson was domineering, cold, and ill-tempered, but he had a great influence on young Hetty, particularly her early ambition to accumulate wealth. The business acumen she developed was not from any Quaker boarding or Boston finishing school education, but from the tutelage of a father whom she followed along the New Bedford waterfront wharves, warehouses, commissaries to the stone and brick office of the family firm. Instead of reading novels or poetry, her printed word originated from newspaper financial pages. Hetty came to abhor New England society and to eschew the traditional trappings of a young woman from a prestigious family. Her preoccupation was with money, and it was evident by the time she was in her early 20s.

A Battle of Wills. Hetty recognized that the fastest route to the family wealth was through inheritance, and like a vulture eyeing carrion, she anticipated the expiration of her mother, grandfather, father, and – most famously – her aunt Sylvia Ann Howland. Eager for their fortunes, she was mostly disappointed by the sums left to her in their wills. While most of America was engrossed in the final years of the nation's Civil War, Hetty Robinson was, instead, immersed in the pursuit of the last wealthy family member to die, her aunt Sylvia.

In December 1865, Hetty produced a will very different from Sylvia's probated version. It was dubious enough that Hetty was the primary beneficiary of the new edition, but more suspicious was the appearance of an unwitnessed second page, complete with a Sylvia signature. If Hetty's will was proven a forgery, she would at best lose the battle – at worst she could be charged with a felony. The ensuing contest, held in the US Circuit Court of Massachusetts, was widely watched across New England. Seven attorneys toiled to prove the validity of Hetty's version against three for the probate trustees.

Both sides produced a litany of experts, their study and testimony spanning months. Harvard University was called upon to provide many of the authorities. One was a chemist who analyzed the ink composition of the unwitnessed signatures on the second will. Another, renowned mathematician Charles Peirce, reduced the signature's pen strokes to probabilities. Naturalist Louis Agassiz, Chairman of Harvard's Department of Natural History, added science to the hearings with his microscopy of ink and paper at "a power exceeding thirty diameters." Harvard lawyer Oliver Wendell Holmes Jr. debated the finer points of the case. In addition to the luminaries, there were forensic photographers, engravers, penmanship professionals, and tracing experts. In all, 16 expert testimonies were called on the prosecution side and for the defense, a dozen.

Thirty-three-year-old Hetty married 46-year-old Edward Henry Green in 1867. Before a walk down the aisle, it was understood that he had no rights to her money. After their honeymoon, the bride and groom moved to England awaiting the outcome of Hetty's very public legal fight. Two children were born to the Green's in London – Edward Howland Robinson, who was born in 1868, and Harriet Sylvia Ann, born in 1871. When Hetty's petition in the Aunt Sylvia case was dismissed on a technicality, and the matter was quietly settled during her appeal to the United States Supreme Court, the Green's returned to America.

Hetty's Good Fortune. While Hetty Green prospered during the 1870s and 80s by investing in the undervalued US dollar, bonds, and railroads, her husband Edward's finances declined during the Panic of 1873 and again in 1885. The second time he lost more than just money.

In 1885, Hetty Green was the largest creditor of the brokerage firm of John J. Cisco & Son. But the once cautious institution was teetering on the edge of collapse and her husband, who had used Hetty's bankroll as collateral on his investments, was the firm's largest debtor. To cover his obligations, her only recourse was to forfeit $700,000 – about $21 million today.

Hetty never forgave her husband, who, in the words of Peter Wyckoff, she disposed of "as quickly as she would have sold any dubious investment." When the Green's relocated to New York, Ned's father took one apartment, while Hetty, Ned, and his sister Sylvia moved to another in Brooklyn. Now, with only short visits to see his father, Ned was raised mostly by his mother.

America was fascinated with the eccentricities, parsimony, and financial genius of Hetty Green. One of the most discussed idiosyncrasies was her fashion. The most popular image of her was as a dour, hurried woman garbed in an ankle-length black dress that was sewn from "practically indestructible material," her accouterments comprising a flowing black cape, long bonnet, and an oversized handbag that, it was rumored, was filled with tens of thousands of dollars and, later in life, a pistol.

Hetty hated lawyers, doctors, and the taxman. She called lawyers buzzards and refused to pay for their services until they sued her. When Hetty acquired a permit to carry her pistol, one newspaper declared that her intention was "to shoot lawyers who may become obstreperous in her presence." Doctors fared little better – to Hetty, they "were a bunch of robbers." Rather than pay for a hernia operation, she stuffed a stick between her clothing and abdomen to apply pressure to the afflicted area. The pain she suffered for 20 years was evidently preferable to paying for doctor fees.

Hetty Green never claimed a permanent residence, in part because of the expense, but mostly to avoid paying property taxes. She relocated to different cities and towns often, her children sharing cold-water flats, rented apartments, hotel rooms, and boarding houses in Manhattan, Brooklyn, Long Island, Boston, Morristown, and Hoboken, New Jersey. Her subterfuges included signing her pet terrier Dewey's name on real estate transactions, leases, and the nameplate of various apartments. Hetty, whose net worth put her in the same circles as the Gould's, Carnegie's, Morgan's, and Rockefeller's was more interested in evading state tax coffers than she was in palatial residences.

Stories abounded about penny-pincher Hetty Green. She was known to avoid the menu items of most New York restaurants she frequented, ordering only crackers or a cheap, simple broth, then departing without a tip for the wait staff. During her 14-hour workdays, she habitually ate oatmeal from a pot heated on the radiators of her Wall Street office at the Chemical National Bank. The porridge gave her the strength, she said, to "fight those Wall Street wolves." When Hetty commissioned a studio photograph of Ned as a boy, she pressed only the front of his crumpled suit – it was senseless to spend money on the part of his wardrobe not in the photograph. To avoid the expense of fresh flowers in her dwellings, she shaped them herself from paper or dyed chicken feathers.

In Arthur Lewis's account, the eccentric woman who was known as much for her intelligence as "biting sarcasm and

16

sharp temper" and "cold, hard stares" was also a financial genius. Over her life, she accumulated tens of millions of dollars in securities, mortgages, railroad bonds, municipal bonds, California mines, and real estate that spread across New England, Chicago, St. Louis, and Cincinnati. The sums she gave to charity were small, her only documented gifts to humanity were the offer of loans at below-market rates to city works projects and churches.

Hetty's triumph in the male-dominated business world was no minor accomplishment. A voracious reader and researcher of the financial markets, she possessed a "surpassing shrewdness and foresight." In her business transactions, those who sat across the bargaining table from Hetty Green remember her as fearless, at times ruthless. A minister of the Fifth Presbyterian Church of Chicago told Hetty that, if she foreclosed on its loan, she would go to hell. Hetty foreclosed. From the pulpit, the minister dedicated his entire last sermon to the vilification of Hetty Green.

When Hetty Green made an enemy in business she went to great lengths to exact revenge. At the top of her long list of adversaries was railroad and shipping magnate Collis Potter Huntington, the builder of America's first transcontinental railroad. If she was able to avoid expletives in references to him, he was either "the old hyena" or the "devil Huntington." She once threatened to shoot him in a business meeting, the hazard real enough to send him scurrying for the door. Huntington was always on the wrong side of Hetty Green, but his most egregious failing, in her eyes, was his mismanagement of the Huntington-owned Houston & Texas Central Railway (H&TC).

Part of Huntington's strategy to dominate the Texas railroad industry was by consolidating several existing, but largely failing, short line tracks. Not satisfied with just a monopoly, he increased ownership of more than a few by forcing them into receivership, then buying back shares at distressed prices from rattled investors anxious to sell. One of the bankrupted Huntington lines was the H&TC, and Hetty Green was one of its largest investors. To make matters worse, Huntington's H&TC railroad debt contributed, in part, to the fall of the John J. Cisco & Son firm – the repository that held most of Hetty's cash and securities, and her husband Edward's debt.

Hetty, the financial tactician, set a trap. While others panicked, she accumulated Huntington's depressed H&TC's bonds as quickly as they became available. Hetty next declared she would support the railroad's reorganization plan, then surprised everyone by foreclosing on her portion of the mortgage bonds. Her business prize was a piece of Huntington's H&TC, but the non-monetary reward was priceless. Hetty denied the move was retribution, it was simply a defense against Huntington the baron robber who was trying to squeeze her out of the railroad business. "You can go to bed at night with a railroad," she quipped, "and wake up in the morning to find Huntington had stolen it."

Hetty's Son. Ned Green was four years old when the family returned from England to Bellows Falls, Vermont, in 1872. His childhood was not like most wealthy New Englanders of the era. He and his sister Sylvia were often objects of curiosity, mostly due to the contradiction between their mother's immense wealth and her spendthrift reputation, odd dress, and mannerisms. Both of her children wore second-hand clothing that, Arthur Lewis wrote, were "sometimes lined with papers to keep out the cold."

Young Ned was involved in a sledding mishap that left him lame in one leg, and it was the start of a handicap that persisted for the rest of his life. Sister Sylvia dragged him to school in a cart. Physically unable to join in, he spent hours watching other children play baseball. Alone, he often hobbled to the banks of the Connecticut River to fish.

Ned was 17 when he enrolled in St. John's College, arriving at the institution in a second-hand suit, selected by his mother, and too small for his 150-pound frame. His formal education lasted about a year. Part of the reason for the short collegiate tenure was his bad leg. There is no agreement between historians on the injury, but one popular version is that Ned –

still walking with a limp from his childhood accident – was struck by an express wagon in 1886 after his first college year. The wound refused to heal as his mother, who declined to pay for proper treatment, towed him to charitable medical clinics across New York.

Ned's leg developed gangrene, the infection threatening his life. It may have been his father who stepped in and paid for an amputation of the left leg above the knee. A year later the leg finally healed and Ned was fitted with a cork prosthetic. The separated limb was buried in the Bellows Falls family cemetery.

Fifteen hundred miles away, a scrawny black farm boy named Bill McDonald left the picking fields of Texas, walking 600 miles to Tennessee with the dream of attending college. In Illinois, a blossoming 15-year-old redhead by the name of Mabel Harlow was beginning to attract the attention of the opposite sex. It was the mid-1880s, and at that moment the likelihood of either of these people, much less a rusting 51-mile stretch of the H&TC railroad, converging to play pivotal roles in the life of a recuperating Ned Green seemed entirely unlikely.

Ocean-going sailing ships, barrels of whale oil, and railroad tracks at the New Bedford waterfront. Edward Mott Robinson's business office was nearby where he taught his daughter, Hetty, the ways of business and finance. Courtesy New Bedford Free Public Library, Joseph G. Tirrell Photograph Collection, https://ark.digital commonwealth.org /ark:/50959 /mk61t4129.

Hetty Green and her dog Dewey, that probably owned more real estate and other investments – at least on paper – than any other dog, at the time, in the world. Courtesy of Boston Public Library, Leslie Jones Collection, No.08-06-009231, https://ark.digitalcommonwealth.org/ark:/50959/5x21t m02s.

A portrait of railroad capitalist E.H.R. Green in 1895. Green became the youngest railroad president in the United States, at age 24, when he was named president of the Texas Midland Railroad. The genial, enthusiastic, and considerate gentleman made friends everywhere and was warmly respected by the officers and employees of the railroad. He often joined the engineer at the front of the train, holding the throttle of the engine during trips down the line where, sometimes donning overalls, he visited towns and employees of his depots and machine shops. Collection of Jim Moloney.

CHAPTER 3

BEING E.H.R. GREEN

On the eve of his 20th birthday, Ned Green was rudderless. His leg had healed, but with an artificial limb, he walked with a noticeable limp. Ned was admitted to the bar but decided, instead, on the railroad business, working for a short time as a clerk at the Connecticut River Railroad Company and the Ohio and Mississippi Railroad. Determined to provide him with some direction, Hetty packed the 21-year-old off to Chicago to run part of her real estate empire.

The son of the richest woman in America checked into his Windy City hotel holding a briefcase patched together with twine and wearing his customary poorly fitted, thrift shop suit. Although he made friends easily and was invited to join several social organizations, he still lacked self-confidence. Partly it was his unusual upbringing, partly his handicap, and certainly his discomfort around women. His newfound Chicago friends reckoned that Ned didn't suffer from anything that couldn't be cured by sex. They were right.

Chicago. The brothel was lavish, its ladies alluring in their cosmetics, perfume, and fineries. As Ned drank in the scene, he knew they were unlike any other women that, until now, he had watched from afar. One, with red hair, was as enchanting as she was seasoned. Her name was Mabel Harlow. Her resume was lengthy, having worked the men's convention circuit across the Midwest and the South, marrying several men for just short durations, then always returning to her occupation. Ned lost his virginity to Mabel. Then he fell in love with her. When she scampered off to California in 1892 with yet another fleeting paramour, Ned returned to New York.

Hetty would have sent for her son anyway. Ned had watched his mother manipulate the press to her business benefit with great skill. But in Chicago, he showed he lacked her maturity. When reporters penned Ned's pronouncements for the opening of a new Green company headquarters, a bank, and even a newspaper, he had overplayed his hand. It was bad enough that none of his proclamations was true. What bothered Hetty most, however, was that this, his first step from under her long shadow, confirmed he was not ready.

Hetty reigned Ned in, then sent him to Texas. The year was 1892, and 24-year-old Ned was about to become the youngest railroad president in the United States. As noble as the title appeared on paper, the reality was less lofty. His trophy was a decrepit short line railroad, originally a piece of Huntington's H&TC. Hetty's was a calculated risk. If Ned failed, she would lose little more than 51 miles of an unprofitable, underutilized railroad. If he succeeded, it might ready him to one day navigate the Hetty Green business empire. But as he left New York City for Terrell, Texas on that cold December 1892 day, Hetty wasn't placing any bets on which way Ned would go.

Terrell, Texas. It was the Christmas season when railroad president Ned Green walked, with his characteristic limp, into the American National Bank of Terrell. Depositing his mother's $500,000 railroad check, the sum doubled the depository's resources. He was immediately named the bank's vice president. Ned leased a small apartment, intent on reinventing not only the recently renamed Texas Midland Railroad Company (TMR) but the image of Edward Howland Robinson Green.

Ned Green's upbringing in New England could hardly have prepared him for the East Texas town of Terrell, located some 29 miles east of Dallas. First, there was the geography – the town rose from mostly flatland, its landscape brown in winter but verdant green during scorching, humid summers. Then there was the culture. Ned had grown up with Yankee puritanism and learned to navigate the urban environment of two of America's largest cities. But nothing in his life to this point compared to a small town of Bible Belt Baptist churchgoers. Now, removed from his domineering mother's influence, the once introverted teenager was, at last, liberated. The town of Terrell would be less than amused.

Ned, the boy who grew up in unassuming housing and wore secondhand suits, discovered himself in Terrell. He began to appreciate the finer things that money could buy – fine accommodations, silk neckties and tailored suits, imported food, wine, and cigars, and women. Surrounding himself with a "devoted band of revelers," he spent lavishly on the nighttime circuit of Dallas and Terrell hotels, restaurants, and clubs. He had become gregarious and garrulous, and instead of eschewing the limelight, embraced it. At 6-foot-4 and weighing over 200 pounds, Ned commanded the attention he now craved whenever he entered a room. Named one of America's most eligible bachelors, he was portrayed as "fond of athletic exercises" and had gained "the iron muscles of a well-developed specimen of hardy manhood."

There were some in Terrell who began to judge the moral character of that specimen of hardy manhood with increasing disdain. Eyebrows were first raised when, in 1894, Ned abandoned his spartan apartment and rebuilt the expansive top floor of the Harris Opera House. Occupied with several of his male friends, the extravagant bachelor quarters of the "Green Flat," as it was called, was suspect for its decadence. A procession of young women, often of questionable repute, paraded through the Green Flat door where, it was said, Ned could best be located through the smoke and booze bottles by following a trail of discarded prosthetic cork legs. When the bachelors finally moved out, Terrell's polite society noted that the Yankee railroader seemed to settle into a more socially acceptable routine, attended by only his housekeeper. It wouldn't take long before the town learned her identity – former Chicago prostitute Mabel Harlow.

The Texas Midland. Part of Ned's newfound self-confidence was gained by his success at the helm of his newly minted railroad. The rusting railroad that began at "nowhere and ended at the same place" was in receivership when Ned took charge. One journalist portrayed its track as a "roadbed overgrown with grass and weeds" its "small rails rusty for want of use" and its "rolling stock dropping to pieces, the ancient-looking locomotives too weak to draw a good breath of steam." Along with its sagging wooden bridges, wrecks were so common along the line that Dallas newspaperman William G. Sterrett dubbed it "the angel-maker."

Ned put the same amount of energy into the railroad industry that he did in pursuing the good life. He became a committed student of the subject, reading books and magazines, and asking questions of everyone around him. He was unrelenting in his drive to turn the TMR into a profitable company. In the first years, Ned pumped $2 million into the business, laying heavy-gauge rails and ties over a roadbed ballasted with fireclay, replacing wooden bridges with steel. Depots were replaced, including one he named the Harlow. The original 51 miles of track was extended to 125 miles, with Ned negotiating contracts to build connections at both terminations with other carriers.

New locomotives and passenger cars were ordered, all designed with the most modern technology of the times. Ned's TMR was the first company to install electric lights on its engines, and he purchased steel boxcars and high-speed gas and electric railcars. One train Ned procured, the *Lone Star Limited*, was unveiled to the press at an exhibition in St. Louis. The media gushed over its oak-trimmed coach cars, the first lit solely by "acetylene gas" that made it "possible to read with ease."

Then came the *Lone Star Special* with its opulent, state-of-the-art lounge cars and observation sleepers. Ned commissioned George Pullman, president of the Pullman Palace Car Company, to design a special parlor car for the train. It was the most elegant ever constructed, complete with easy chairs that graced three staterooms. Painted maroon, Ned presented it as a gift to his consort, Mabel Harlow.

The maroon car with the name Mabel painted in gold on its sides steamed into Terrell at the end of its maiden trip. Ned, expecting to be met with the usual horde of reporters and onlookers that marked each of his achievements, was instead greeted by the city marshal. The people of Terrell "were offended by his open squiring of a whore," he was told. Mabel would leave town, or she would be arrested.

A Redhead in Dallas. Ned quietly registered Mabel under the alias 'Mrs. Staunton' at the Grand Windsor Hotel in Dallas. But Dallas and the Windsor were no more tolerant than Terrell, and Mabel was moved to the Oriental Hotel before an exasperated Ned bought a house in the city that was, in one writer's words a "gaudy palace with plate glass windows of unusual design, heavy doors, high ceilings, numerous bathrooms, and other elaborate embellishments." In his 1984 Dallas Magazine article, Tom Peeler wrote that mothers with their children would cross the street to avoid the place.

Ned's mother Hetty, the bible quoting Quaker, could not have been more opposite in character than her son's prostitute companion, who she usually referred to as "Miss Harlot." While she not amused at her son's antics, she remained silent on the subject, at least publicly. And unlike Chicago, this time she did not call him back home.

A Passion for Politics. By the time he was 30 years old, Ned Green was an accomplished railroad man, president of the American National Bank of Dallas, and director of nearly a dozen others. The Mabel Harlow scandal had little impact on his growing fortune, but earlier, Ned set his sights on another Texas prize – a prestigious political position. Here, Hetty's "Miss Harlot" was a liability, and it made him an easy target for conservative politicians. His judgment was also questionable on another critical topic – his choice of political parties. Ned Green was a stalwart Republican, "a hopeless party" in the Lone Star State. Ned Green – known mostly now as Eddie to his friends and E.H.R. Green in business – would find his political ambitions elusive.

When E.H.R. Green decided to make his political mark as a Republican, he was surely aware that, in a state still resonating with Old South sentimentality, the party of Lincoln was a dead-end for any public office aspirant. In the half-century between 1845 and the 1896 election, for example, only two of Texas's 21 governors were Republicans. It was also a party divided. The progressive 'Black and Tans' faction courted the black vote and found a place for African Americans within its ranks. The 'Lily Whites,' while acknowledging the power of the black vote, held sacrosanct that the only face of the party could be white.

Green probably underestimated the impact that his moral lapses and racial tolerance would have on his state political ambitions. But as he threw his hat into the ring, he was certainly astute enough to recognize the growing importance of the Lone Star State to the Republican party at the national level, and its influence on federal patronage to Texas. It was a calculated risk.

E.H.R. Green was only 28 years old when he set his sights on the governor's seat. Some say his mother, who announced she would "spend a million to gratify his ambitions," convinced him to enter politics. Others believe it was William (Bill) "Gooseneck" McDonald. The son of slaves, McDonald earned a college degree before a future that included banking, the Masons, and Republican politics. By the mid-1890s, McDonald, it was written, was "the strongest and most popular colored man of the party in Texas." Bill and Ned remained politically aligned for the next nearly ten years.

Green's political rise was meteoric. He had been in Texas less than four years before announcing for governor. Up to that point, his only involvement in the Lone Star Republican party was a minor role as 6th District Representative in the Republican League. Although the Lily Whites blocked him from winning the gubernatorial nomination that year, he won the 1896 chairmanship of the state Republican Executive Committee by a large margin. His detractors accused him of buying the position with money deftly dispensed to party delegates by Bill McDonald, or in the words of writer William Bryk, he "overwhelmed the state convention in a tidal wave of babes, booze, and gold."

The political success Green achieved was, in part, orchestrated by his mother, who traveled to Washington to lobby national party leaders on his behalf. According to writer Janet Wallach, Hetty recreated her image for the political occasion, surrendering her traditional garb for "the finest sort of a dress." Uncharacteristically, she lodged at the most expensive hotel in town, the Shoreham, and "never asked the rate." Wallach wrote that Hetty's words and money had the desired outcome.

For his part, E.H.R. Green electrified the party. Texas had managed only 80,000 votes for the 1892 Republican presidential candidate, but the number leaped to 167,000 under Ned's leadership during the 1896 campaign. When he produced on his promise to deliver the Lone Star State's electoral votes to presidential contender William McKinley, he was rewarded for his efforts with a place in McKinley's inauguration parade astride a white stallion.

The summer heat was punishing on that August day in 1898 as a network of trains dispatched some 400 GOP delegates to the Republican state convention in Fort Worth. Disembarking from his private Pullman car, party chairman E.H.R. Green was greeted with a brass band and a throng of well-wishers. Newsmen followed Ned and the other arriving party leaders as they retired to their respective hotel rooms, anxious to capture their moods and words. They weren't particularly interested in the party manifesto. Mostly, they wanted to know the names of the candidates on the state ticket. They knew that the Republicans were bracing for a fight.

The list for governor was long. Judge Harry Cline from Harris County and San Antonio's Colonel George W. Brackenridge were both early favorites, and there was talk again of Green running for the top spot. Support for Green faded fast, however, when the convention learned that even his reelection to the state chairmanship was questionable. At issue was the Lily White's objection to Bill McDonald as temporary chairman. Crosscurrents of intrigue pitted Green and McDonald against a growing number of Lily White supporters. In the end, Green with the Black and Tans managed to triumph, but the fight made him lasting political foes.

Green would continue to pursue politics for the foreseeable future, but that summer he was only too pleased to put his ambitions behind him. Two months earlier, he had decided on a site to construct the most lavish sporting club the nation had ever seen. He was heading to the Texas coast.

E.H.R. "Ned" Green, formally named Edward Howland Robinson Green, was the creative genius behind the Tarpon Club. The son of Hetty Green, popularly known as the "Witch of Wall Street," the richest woman in the United States. Green was named president of the Texas Midland Railroad Company by his mother at age 24 in 1893. In 1896 he became active in Texas Republican Party politics. The next year he laid plans to build the exclusive Tarpon Club on St. Joseph Island, its clubhouse completed in early 1899. Library of Congress, Prints & Photographs Division, ggbain 05302 //hdl.loc.gov/loc.pnp/ggbain.05302, https://lccn.loc.gov/2014685295.

Advertisement for E.H.R. Green's Texas Midland Railroad. Collection of Jim Moloney.

Railroad passes, which allowed their holders to travel at no cost as far and as often as they liked, were eagerly sought by businessmen and politicians. Revealing a side of him not unlike his mother, E.H.R. detested providing these "charity passes." Shown is a Texas Midland Railroad pass from 1907, issued to Mexia's W.J. Bryant, a local and state politician from Limestone County. Note the facsimile signature of E.H.R. Green, President & General Manager in the lower right-hand corner. Texas Midland Railroad Pass, 1907; University of North Texas Libraries, The Portal to Texas History, crediting Hardin-Simmons University Library, https://texashistory. unt.edu/ark:/67531/metapth1091525/.

E.H.R. Green's private railroad car. Collection of Jim Moloney.

The Texas Midland Railroad Depot in Greenville, Texas, built by E.H.R. Green in the early 1900s. Collection of Jim Moloney.

34

CHAPTER 4

THE AMERICAN SPORTSMAN

America at the end of the 19th century was basking in industrial and financial prosperity. These were heady times for men in professions such as law, medicine, and politics, but particularly for finance and business. It was the era of unregulated banking and investing, and they were making up the rules as they went. The most successful players possessed not just ambition, intellect, and courage but unusual cunning, greed, and ruthlessness.

Many from the halls of power were outdoorsmen. Some were gentleman sportsmen and conservationists, while others conveyed the same approach to sporting activities that they did to business. For them, time afield was less about leisure than a competition to bag the largest volume, rarest, biggest, or most dangerous game fish or animal. Part of the attraction of their fishing and hunting exploits was certainly the challenge and thrill of the chase. Part of it was that – much like a financial statement – what they killed or caught was measurable.

Leisure was made possible not just from financial resources, but from advancements in technology. Railroad tracks now crisscrossed the continent, allowing for rapid travel to formerly remote parts of the countryside via comfortable dining and sleeping cars. Steam had replaced sails on America's waterways, and gasoline engines would make their appearance by the end of the century. Improvements in the outdoorsmen's tools also played a role, notably in firearms and fishing tackle, that made it possible to kill or catch larger numbers and bigger trophies.

Shotgunning. Firearms developed rapidly between the Civil War and the early 20th century. Inefficient and cumbersome black powder muzzleloaders were superseded during the late 1870s by breech-loading, hammerless shotguns. Some of the world's finest European and American side-by-side shotguns were produced by dozens of gunmakers during the era, and they became the staple of every shotgunning gentleman. Smokeless powder, factory-loaded shotgun shells, and mass-produced, repeating shotguns made their appearance in the late 1800s.

The name John M. Browning was sacrosanct among sportsmen owing to his development of the Winchester slide-action pump Model 1893 and its successor the 1897, followed by the first semi-automatic shotgun, the Browning A-5, in 1902. The combination of pre-loaded 'white smokeless powder' shotgun shells and the five-shot pump and semi-automatic shotguns became the arsenal of choice for nearly all monied sportsmen and commercial gunners.

Advancements in shotgunning technology led to the popularization of an innovative, new sport – wing shooting. The time-consuming logistics required for loading early weapons made it impractical to do anything other than fire into flocks of game birds on the water or land. With breech-loaders and factory-produced shotgun ammunition, sportsmen took up the challenge of hitting moving targets. Competitive shooting with live pigeons and thrown glass ball targets was quickly popularized, as well as hunting wild birds on the wing.

Wing shooters, who usually measured their success in the volume of birds killed, were always in search of the next untouched frontier to pursue their passion. America's waterfowl hunters had already witnessed the decline of the once-fabled East Coast fowling grounds, a result of proximity to populated eastern seaboard cities with too many sport and market gunners pursuing a finite resource. For wing shooters in *the late 1800s, the new frontier was the Texas Gulf Coast.

36

In 1893, *Field and Stream* magazine proclaimed that "Texas today is the finest and best hunting and fishing ground in the United States." Another periodical heralded the Gulf Coast as "the greatest sporting discovery of the age." The Texas Coastal Bend was mentioned often, such as the glowing testimony that Aransas Bay had the "finest hunting and fishing on the continent," with "canvasback and redhead ducks in abundance." America's monied wing shooters were quick to follow the advice.

Big Game Fishing. Prior to 1880, there was no such sport as big game fishing. Large game fish, if they were targeted at all, were caught by hand lines. In hand-lining, an airtight keg was attached to a rope, chain, line, and thick steel hook, the barrel acting as a float to "retard and even stop the fish." Then a small boat was rowed to the tiring prey, the chase ending with a carefully placed harpoon. When the first tales of giant fish caught on rod and reel began to circulate, a new sporting game was born. The fever spread quickly.

Big game saltwater fishing with rod and reel got its start with tarpon in 1885, its birthplace the remote Florida Gulf Coast. The rise in tarpon fishing popularity was hard to fathom. It was a fish that had no value on the epicurean's table, and its only known haunt – the west coast of Florida – was a very hard destination to reach during the late 1800s, requiring a trip by rail, horse and buggy, and steamers or sailing vessels. There were few hotels, but an abundance of mosquitoes and rattlesnakes, although most destinations were, by then, "free from yellow fever."

According to game-fishing historian Ed Pritchard, no one believed it was possible to catch a fish over 100 pounds on conventional fishing tackle. That changed in 1880 when Samuel M. Jones landed a 130-pound tarpon using tackle developed for New England striped bass. Five years later, William Halsey Wood landed another tarpon over 100 pounds. His feat, covered by *Forest and Stream* magazine, was the ember that ignited the tarpon craze. Wood's fish was followed by a record-breaking 184-pound tarpon landed by New York angler John G.

Hecksher in St. James City, Florida, a feat considered so remarkable that he presented the specimen to the Smithsonian Institute.

In 1896, after Charles Frederic Holder landed the first tuna that weighed over a 100 pounds on rod and reel, the fishing world turned its attention to marlin, sailfish, and swordfish. By the end of the century, big game fishing evolved into one of the fastest-growing sports in America. As with shotgunning, anglers relied on technological advancements in tackle to continue to push the boundaries of the sport. The list of improvements impacted everything from reels, rods, lines, leaders, to hooks.

Before the use of the multiplying, or casting reel, early reels were little more than a repository for excess line. Reel advancements during the early tarpon era came mostly from New York City, home to the makers of the finest brass or German silver reel on the market. The names of Edward vom Hofe, his father, and brothers Friedrich and Julius vom Hofe, Thomas J. Conroy, J.B. Crook & Co., and John Kopf were soon known to every serious angler. As the prey grew bigger so did the reels they made. Larger reels were developed to carry as much as 300 yards of line and take the strain of a big fish, evolving from the workhorse 4/0 category to a 10/0 size, then rapidly reaching the bulk of a 16/0.

Early tarpon reels did not have a clutch or friction drag. The tension required to slow the dash of a powerful fish – and prevent it from stripping all the line from the reel – was applied by hand using a thumb stall. Attached to the back of the reel and made of leather strips, the best from moosehide, the thumb stall was all that prevented the line from ripping through an angler's cotton glove or shearing the skin from their hand. Because there were no anti-reverse mechanisms on early reels, handles tended to spin backward while fighting a fish, resulting in broken knuckles and fingers. When Edward vom Hofe engineered the first modern internal friction style drag in 1902, he revolutionized big game fishing. Even so, anglers sometimes poured water on early friction reels to reduce heat while battling a fish.

Fishing rods, as prone to failure as early reels, commonly snapped when too much pressure was applied to a big fish. Rods, typically about six to seven feet long, were initially made from bamboo, ash, greenheart, noibwood, or hickory, and they were often brittle. Rod makers continued to strive for a balance of strength with tractability. Among the greatest improvements were vom Hofe's solid hickory rod, another built of six-sided, split bamboo, and experimentation with new blanks made of ironwood or lancewood.

The metal sleeves that held the rod sections together, called ferrules, were another weak point. If the ferrules did not shatter, failure might occur on one of the guides. Early rod guides included a ring soldered to a metal collar and bell guides that were wrapped around the rod with thread or twine. These evolved into rods that were fitted with high-quality nickel components, raised tunnel bridge guides, and silver roller tips.

Finally, there were the rod's grip and reel seat locks. By the late 1800s, rod grips advanced from cork to a stronger braided cord or celluloid. Reel seats, however, remained a vulnerability, and the best option was simply to lash the reel to the rod. Beyond the rod and reel, fish were lost when the line broke, leaders parted, and hooks failed, either because a fish straightened them entirely, or they shattered like glass.

When anglers first chased tarpon their only fishing line option was commercially available "Black Bass" line. It wasn't up to the task. Manufacturers hurriedly experimented with variations such as twisted or braided silk or cotton. Early fishing line, regardless of its composition, had to be stripped from the reel and dried after each day on the water. The development of linen Cuttyhunk line modernized big game fishing line. Expert anglers favored the lighter 15-strand line, while the heavier 24-strand Cuttyhunk was more suited for the novice.

The selection of material that attached hook to the line – the leader – was more critical in tarpon sport fishing than any other saltwater game fishing. Leaders were first made from piano wire. Not only did the wire break – either from the fight of the fish or the impact of its hard jaws – but fish were easily spooked by the unnatural attachment of bait to wire.

The solution was a flexible line between the hook and the wire leader, termed a snell. Early experiments with cotton cord, stout cod-line, and moose snood were followed by the introduction of braided flax with enough threads such that a fish could not easily gnaw them through. After the turn of the century, experts advised attaching braided snells to "phosphor-bronzed" wire leaders "at least five feet in length and divided into three lengths and connected by swivels."

Hook quality was judged solely by the ability to stand up to the rigors of the game, and for hook manufacturers, nothing was superior to tempered, forged steel. The preferred tarpon hook was a size 10/0, three inches long. Among the best known were those marketed by O'Shaughnessy, imported English bronze and Limerick hooks, or those made in Ohio by Van Vleck with the barbs situated outside of the hook rather than the inside.

Equipment might have kept anglers in the game, but it was hyperbole that brought them there in the first place. Their prey, the tarpon, was depicted in phrases such as "fluid poetry," and "shimmering, silver-sided royalty," the "Silver King of game fish," and a trophy "devilishly sly and of uncanny awareness" that "tests the nerves, the judgment, and the strength of the sportsman." Skillful anglers estimated that, of the fish that rose to their bait, only one fish in four could be hooked, and of those, only one in four was landed.

Those who witnessed a school of tarpon hitting live baitfish described a spectacle of erupting water and aerial acrobatics, a seeming celebration of the chase and the kill. It was an exhibition impossible for fishermen to imitate at the end of a rod and reel – dead bait simply did not replicate the theatrics of a tarpon's normal feeding habit. According to A.W. Dimock, the first tarpon bait was a hook ingeniously sewn inside half a mullet. But tarpon, if the least bit mistrustful, knowingly flung hooks and bait from their mouth.

There were rules to catching the majestic silver king, unwritten at first. The sportsman waiting for a strike loosely coiled some 30 to 40-feet of line at their feet. When the tarpon first took the bait, practiced fishermen set the hook only after the uncoiled line was taken up. Then they struck hard to set the hook. When fighting the fish, the best custom was to drop and aim the tip of the rod in front of wherever they thought the fish was headed. That sounded easier than it was. After its strike, the silver king might run for shallow water, or head to sea. On a single run, it could strip out hundreds of feet of line, the angler's reel too hot to touch from the friction.

Tarpon provided a fight that, in some instances, lasted for four to five hours. The contest had its own vernacular – the forward roll was called greyhounding, the aerial displays termed jack-knifing. The moments that the tarpon propelled itself from the sea were not only breathtaking but presented the most risk for the trophy to eject hook and bait by "shaking itself with violent contortions" while throwing and rolling its head. The fish only admitted surrender when, at last, it rolled over on its side.

Once landed, the tarpon was gaffed. Then, the heavy metallic scales that lined the great fish were removed, and on several, the fish's weight, length, and the name of the angler carefully scribed. When the bragging was done, the carcass was used for fertilizer. The killing of the fish was later considered unthinkable, but only after the once unheard-of feat of landing a tarpon on rod and reel became more commonplace.

Little was known about the great game fish in the early days. It was considered mysterious, its habitats puzzling. At the turn of the century, the tarpon's range was still unknown, recorded only on the west coast of Florida, then Pensacola, the Texas Coastal Bend, and in Tampico, Mexico. Early pundits suggested that tarpon were migratory, and that water temperature might be a factor in their distribution. In Texas, the fish wasn't even called a tarpon, it was the "savanilla" or "grand ecaille." Experts of the day observed that tarpon were "very numerous on some points on the coast of Texas, notably Corpus

Christi and Lavaca bays," but erroneously added that "they are seldom if ever found" anywhere else.

The first Texas reference to tarpon sport fishing was in the *Galveston Daily News*, in 1885, which carried a feature on Florida tarpon fishing reprinted from the *New York Times*. For the next five years, Texas newspapers only followed the pursuit of tarpon in Florida waters. That changed with a San Antonio fishing party in 1890. Targeting the silver king along the Corpus Christi Bay shoreline of Flour Bluff, two anglers raised several fish, but failed to land them. Their rods, "fitted for only bass" snapped, and lines broke. The exception was banker J.S. Lockwood. Lockwood, who brought the "latest in tarpon tackle," landed two – one weighing 70 and another 100 pounds.

The news electrified Texas outdoorsmen. "Local sportsmen are much excited," newspapers espoused, adding there was no longer a need to go to Florida. Only days later, the *San Antonio Daily Express* reported that another angling party, armed "with the most improved tarpon outfits," had left for Flour Bluff. Texas tarpon fishing was on the map.

The importance of conservation was only just beginning to enter American vocabulary in the late 1800s. Although history would teach a different lesson, most sportsmen believed the country's natural resources were inexhaustible. A steep decline in wild game and game fish would occur after the turn of the century, the finger-pointing aimed at habitat destruction, too many sportsmen pursuing a limited resource, and advancements and efficiencies of the tools they used. But in 1897, as E.H.R. Green was planning his great sporting club, his every move was consistent with the times. He would cater to the Anglo males at the pinnacle of America's industrial age and ride the wave of abundant waterfowl and game fish. Particularly the silver king.

John M. Browning's improvements to shooting technology were legendary. Shown here are the Browning designed Winchester Model 1897 (top) and its successor repeating pump shotgun, the Model 12 (bottom). Hunting guides in coastal Texas were not only experts on game animals, birds, and fish, they were also skilled sea captains. Note the tenders or "pulling skiffs" behind the wheelhouse of this sailing sloop that were used to transport hunters and gear to shallow water. Courtesy Ted Bates Jr.

Repeating shotguns provided hunters the opportunity to harvest larger numbers of birds before reloading. Christopher Spencer introduced the first repeating pump gun in 1882, followed in quick succession by Winchester's Model 1887 lever-action repeater, John M. Browning's Winchester 1893 pump gun and its successor, the Model 1897, built for smokeless powder. This image is of the celebrated Browning Automatic 5-shot, or simply A-5. The A-5 made its appearance in 1902 and was the first semi-automatic shotgun produced. Browning's semi-automatic used the gun's recoil to transfer shotgun shells from the magazine to the chamber. In contrast, pump shotguns relied on a sliding forearm to cycle ammunition from the magazine to the chamber. Courtesy Palmer and Talley Melton.

SOUTHERN PACIFIC CO.

THE finest hunting and fishing on the Continent can be found on the lines of the SOUTHERN PACIFIC Co. and affiliated lines. **The home of the Tarpon** is at Aransas Pass, Tex. Canvas-back and Red-head Ducks in abundance are there also.

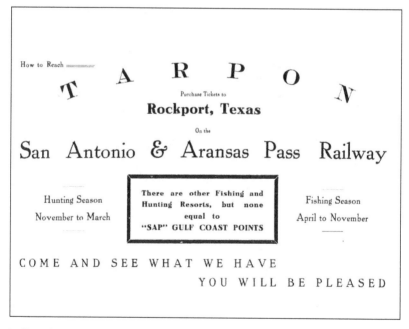

How to Reach

T A R P O N

Purchase Tickets to

Rockport, Texas

On the

San Antonio & Aransas Pass Railway

Hunting Season

November to March

There are other Fishing and Hunting Resorts, but none equal to "SAP" GULF COAST POINTS

Fishing Season

April to November

COME AND SEE WHAT WE HAVE

YOU WILL BE PLEASED

Railroad companies such as the Southern Pacific and SAAP advertised special rates, fitted cars, and other amenities to attract sportsmen. Top image is from *The American Angler*, Vol. 29 No. 6, (New York: Angler's Publishing Co.), 1899; bottom image Collection of Jim Moloney.

45

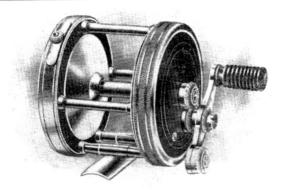

Suggestions for

Winter Fishing

in the South

The " A & I." Noibwood Tarpon
Rod " stands the strain."   Price, $17.50
[Extra tips or any weight to fit the same butt, $8.50 each.]

" A & I." Compensating Tarpon
Reels, from $13.50 to $50.00.

The "A. & I." Tarpon Drag (Rabbeth
Patent) may be put on any reel   It is adjust-
able to any tension.   Price, $7.50

We make tackle for any kind of fishing.   If
you can't call, why not 'phone or write?

Abbey & Imbrie

18 Vesey Street   NEW YORK
[Opposite St. Paul's.]

Telephone, " 4190 Cortlandt."

Advertising the latest advancements in fishing equipment from the
New York firm of Abbey & Imbrie. Collection of Jim Moloney.

46

An early tarpon reel from B. F. Meek & Sons, marketed as the No. 11 tarpon and tuna reel. According to Ed Pritchard, brothers Jonathan and Benjamin Meek were watchmakers in Frankfort, Kentucky during the 1830s. They began crafting casting reels about 1840 before turning to the production of larger reels for striped bass fishing, then graduating to tarpon and tuna reels around the turn of the century. Meek reels were made of hard rubber and German silver and were marked on the bottom of the reel seats with their sizes, no. 7 through 11. The Meeks brother's early big game reels did not yet feature drags or reverse mechanisms. Courtesy Ed Pritchard, https://antiquefishingreels.com/salt-water-reels/meek/#images-1.

Another reel manufactured during the years the Tarpon Club was in operation was built by New Yorker Edward vom Hofe. It featured groundbreaking technology such as a pop-out anti-reverse handle and an internal friction drag. Although the drag could be adjusted with a wrench, it could not be fine-tuned while fighting a fish. Courtesy Ed Pritchard, https://antiquefishingreels.com/big-game-reels/history-evolution/.

CHAPTER 5

CREATING THE TARPON CLUB

The by-laws were written, the $50 annual membership fee was decided, and the ink on the clubhouse architectural drawings was dry. It was early spring of 1898, and the only Tarpon Club item still undecided was the location on which to build. Titans of Texas politics and industry eagerly anticipated the Tarpon Club decision, keenly aware of the economic boost the prestigious club would have on whichever area was chosen. Green savored the speculation. It was free promotion for the club and, perhaps later, voters would be more likely to recognize his name on the governor's ballot.

Galveston, the pearl of the coast, was thought to be favored. Corpus Christi was in the running and Brownsville, a destination still hard to reach because it lacked a railroad, was hopeful. James Fulton of the Coleman-Fulton ranching enterprise upped the ante by offering a stunning bluff location overlooking Aransas Bay near Rockport. A *Forest and Stream* writer recommended the mainland at Live Oak Point on Copano Bay, opining that although far from the fishing, its setting was superior to the barren sand spits "near the channel where the tarpon run" – Aransas Pass.

Green didn't disclose it, but his sights were already set on those barren sand spits, specifically Mustang Island, on the southwest side of the channel between Aransas Bay and the Gulf. Here, a small waterman's town, known first as Ropesville – then more appropriately renamed Tarpon – had already gained a larger-than-life sporting reputation. With a population of about 75, most of whom made a living on the water, its infrastructure consisted of the Seaside Hotel, soon to be renamed the Tarpon Inn, the Aransas lifesaving station, and about 20 cottages scattered among the shifting dunes, oleander, and rose bushes.

That June the Tarpon Club Board of Directors toured Aransas Bay aboard Rockport Captain W.Y. Sedam's yacht *Lady Gay*. When the party returned to Rockport, Ned Green at last announced his decision. The media immediately spread the news. "Hundreds of influential and wealthy sportsmen," one article extolled, "will flock to our Texas fishing and hunting resort in search of recreation, the steam yachts of Eastern millionaires will enliven the bay at Rockport, and the Lone Star State will become famous not only as the Mecca of the health seeker, but the pleasure seeker as well."

No sooner had the *Lady Gay* docked that Green, accompanied by SAAP railway general freight and passenger agent E.J. Martin and club architect E.H. Silven, chartered Captain Sam Gray's "elegant pleasure boat," the *Aeneid*, to survey the selected site. History might have been very different had the club been situated on the original Mustang Island location adjacent to the Seaside Hotel (later renamed the Tarpon Inn). Over the next weeks, however, negotiations stalled. Then they stopped entirely. It was said that the Seaside Hotel failed to acquire its illustrious neighbor because "satisfactory arrangements could not be made with the harbor people." Most thought that there was more to the story, but no one was talking.

In August, Green was back in Rockport and had secured a new deal. Newspapers carried word that the prize would go to the southern tip of St. Joseph Island, opposite the lighthouse, on land owned by Rockport businessmen Richard H. Wood and Sam B. Allyn. There was little surprise when Green selected Rockport, with its railroad connection, hotels, piers, and population of able boat captains, as the port hub for his ambitious club. As soon as the entourage disembarked at Galveston, Western Union wires buzzed with orders for northern mills to begin cutting and shipping lumber.

Green's timing was impeccable. Until the 1880s, travel to the Texas mid-coast had always been demanding, with trips requiring a passage by sea or on land via horse, ox cart, or stagecoach. That changed when the San Antonio & Aransas Pass Railway (SAAP) connected San Antonio to the Coastal Bend towns of Rockport and Corpus Christi, opening a new outdoor magnet to sportsmen from around the world.

The SAAP recognized the value of sportsmen to its business, publishing hunting and fishing reports and featuring special "hunter's tickets" priced at four cents a mile. Their Pullman rail car, the *Isaak Walton*, was specially fitted for sportsmen with kennels, gun racks, a large dining room, parlor, kitchen, and observation room. When E.H.R. Green and his Tarpon Club came to town, the company added a line of sleeping cars on all its trains.

The Tarpon Club was to be the most expensive, expansive, and exclusive club in the world. Although it was completely consistent with other diversions Green would embark on later in his life, it was his first of such mammoth undertakings. Had the Tarpon Club been his only achievement, it still would have made history. The question is why.

A Question of Politics. Before he made his first excursions to the Texas coast in 1895, Ned Green was not much of a sportsman. Perhaps he suddenly developed a passion for fishing and hunting – hurtling himself into a new hobby and carrying it to heights previously unheard of – was entirely consistent with his character.

One Green biographer surmised that the Tarpon Club was a gesture to win the heart of a Texas debutante, but there isn't any evidence to support it. A case can also be made that the club was founded to benefit Ned's railroad business, and the early record tends to support this. On his sporting excursions in the years leading up to the club opening, Ned was always accompanied by business and railroad men. Newspapers dutifully followed their trips, such as an 1896 Rockport outing with brass from the Cotton Belt Railroad that arrived aboard "the finest dining and sleeping cars ever run over the Aransas Pass Road."

The best explanation, however, is that the Tarpon Club was calculated to further Green's political ambitions. While Green would always fete businessmen, in 1897 he shifted his entertaining allegiance to politicians. It started in the spring that year, when Green hosted national political heavyweight Mark A. Hanna, former United States Secretary of the Interior D.R. Francis, and N.B. Swizter, the chairman of the Aransas County Republican Committee, on a Rockport tarpon fishing trip. There is little doubt that their discussion included the subject of Green's plans to build the most elaborate and exclusive club in the world. The unknown is whether, perhaps, his vision was to benefit the national Republican party – and ultimately his place within it – by growing its stake in the South.

Press headlines during promotion before the club's opening could have heralded the nation's famous and wealthy businessmen as newly minted Tarpon Club members. They didn't. Like his mother before him, Green carefully controlled what information was provided to newsmen. When the presses rolled, only the names of national political purebreds were announced. All of them were Republicans.

The list of club members also included many prominent Texas Republicans. Several were past or future candidates for the senate and the governor's chair. Some nine delegates from Green's 1896 Republican state party committees and a large percentage of Texas Republican convention delegates between 1896 and 1904 were on the club's docket. The Tarpon Club was E.H.R. Green's political ticket, and many of the names on its roster were to play pivotal roles in the rise and fall of his aspirations.

A Building in the Sand. As all things E.H.R. Green, the Tarpon Club project moved swiftly. Construction tenders were opened in Dallas only days after the site selection. The carpentry bid went to the Grigsby Construction Co., hardware to M.H. Mahon, Henry Hamilton won the painting and frescoing contract, the lumber and millwork went to R.R.

Godley, and sheet metal and water tanks were under the auspices of the Harris Brothers. Fort Worth's Frank Bulgin had charge of the "plumbing and sanitary arrangements." One of the first orders of business for architect E.H. Silven, who supervised the work, was to construct a telephone line across the bay and connect it to the mainland.

As clubhouse construction progressed, Green ordered a yacht from a Chicago boatyard. Built at the east end of the Erie St. bridge, he attended to every detail of the $14,000 "handsome steam launch." Its 50-foot-long hull and 11-foot beam were constructed of white oak and cypress, with copper plating attached below the waterline. The inside cabin apartment was richly appointed in red plush carpet, silk hangings, and upholstered rocking chairs. Communication between pilot and mechanic, ordinarily initiated by the ringing of a bell, was instead via a modern telephone.

Two 10-hp Simplex naphtha engines delivered a speed of 12 knots on the yacht's Lake Michigan trial run. A pair of auxiliary gasoline engines were installed "for driving a dynamo for lighting the boat" that included a cabin interior illuminated by "eighty incandescent lamps of 16 candle power," a large searchlight on the bow, and "patriotic row of red, white, and blue lights" on the deck roof.

Dubbed the *Mabel*, Green's cruiser was shipped south by rail, connecting at the end of the line to the new Aransas Terminal Railroad and launched on Nov. 16, 1898, at the Morris & Cummings channel behind Harbor Island.

Accompanying Green that fall day on the toffee-colored sand shores of Harbor Island were a handful of his cronies and club members, two women, and some newspapermen. Had the press been more perceptive, they would have realized the story that afternoon wasn't as much the launching as it was the ladies present. One was Mabel Harlow, the other a young consort of Green.

Both women at the ceremony went to great lengths to mislead the media about their identity. Articles in the *Galveston Daily News* and *Brownsville Daily Herald* published Mabel's name as 'Mrs. M.E. Meadow,' and the younger woman as 'Miss Mabel Meadow.' Mabel provided her proper surname to other pressmen, but she still anointed Miss Harlow with her own given name. Green's yacht may have been named for the older Mabel Harlow, but it was the imposter Mabel who christened her. Green and his inner circle undoubtedly relished the ruse.

The man who would pilot the *Mabel* was J. Ed Cotter. The Cotter family lived at Tarpon, the family matron and widow Mary later taking over the Tarpon Inn from Frank Hetfield in the early 1900s. Although a young man, her son Ed had logged as many hours on the water as many graying seamen. When Green sent him by train to his Chicago boatyard to "learn about the combustion and ignition of gasoline engines," it was the first time Ed Cotter had ever left the Coastal Bend.

Work crews stayed in Tarpon during construction while others remained at the worksite. Living mostly in an assortment of tents and small cabins, they endured a harsh environment with clouds of mosquitoes, persistent rattlesnakes, penetrating sun, and stinging sand carried by the wind.

When the last schooner load of cypress lumber was delivered to the southern end of the island across from Aransas Pass, the *Dallas Morning News* gushed that, rising from the sand, was "one of the most beautiful club houses on the continent." Despite the challenges, they had created an architectural and engineering masterpiece.

The two-story, 12,091 square foot cypress and pine wood structure was built on a foundation of 14-foot pilings driven deep into the sand. Built to discerning standards "with as much convenience, luxury, and comforts as may be commanded in [the membership's] own metropolitan homes," the first-floor housed private offices, billiard rooms, the kitchen, dining rooms, and a dance hall with a large open veranda measuring some 42 by 62 feet. On the second floor were 18 "sleeping rooms," ladies and gentlemen bathrooms, two servant quarters, and a parlor "fitted up with an especial view of making ladies comfortable." The interior was finished with matched and beaded wainscoting, its walls covered with mounts of game

54

birds and various fish, including a 175-pound tarpon that measured nearly eight feet, caught by club member C.W. Dawley.

The building's exterior tower and roof gables were shingled in white, the roof red, and the cornice and window trimmings painted in bold green. From the second-floor balcony, stairs led to a 60-foot tower mounted with a formidable searchlight, its roof topped by a 30-foot flagpole from which the club's 15 by 20-foot standard was flown. In total, the clubhouse project consumed nearly half a million board feet of lumber and half a railcar of nails.

In a nod to the future, Green commissioned every modern convenience. Novel copper screens covered each door and window. An electrical plant "containing dynamos run by a naphtha engine" pumped water from a 26,000-gallon cistern through a network of pipes to the building's interior kitchen and bathrooms and was used to power the club's 126 "incandescent lamps" for illumination. The spectacle of the club's lighting was so intense that SAAP passengers on the mainland route between Rockport and Corpus Christi could see the building across the bay at night from the train windows. "Many electric bulbs placed all around the eves of the cupula and wide verandas can be seen for miles," one traveler oozed, "and the effect is bewildering and beautiful."

A wide pier was constructed on the bayside, at its end a large aquarium filled with captive game fish. A tramway was planned that would traverse a mile between the clubhouse and the Gulf to allow guests to easily access the "splendid surf bathing with no seaweed or nettles to bother them." A pavilion and observatory were built "for the convenience of those who wish to observe the sport of angling for the silver king."

There was much speculation on the cost of the Tarpon Club building, fixtures, and furniture, the figure varying widely from a low of $12,000 – $408,000 in today's dollars – to a high of $50,000 – $1.7 million today. Other published figures varied from $15,000, $20,000, to $30,000. Typical for Green, he relished the guesswork and never offered the actual cost.

When the building was complete, the Rockport City Council gathered aboard the *Mabel* on January 8, 1899, to honor Green in a public address. They spoke for all the people of Aransas County, they said, in "tendering our hearty appreciation of your praiseworthy labors in establishing and giving to this locality the magnificent club," adding that they expected it would attract "thousands of the most prominent business and professional men of the country."

A Presidential Opening. In February, a long line of SAAP private cars rolled into Rockport from San Antonio for the formal Tarpon Club opening ceremonies. Among the guests that February were Dallas club members E.M. Reardon, J.S. Armstrong, J.C. O'Connor, and A.P. Cary, with M.L. Eppstein of Denison. Most attending the festivities were accompanied by their wives and children, their names dutifully listed in the proper social columns of the day. Over the next two months, 228 members and guests traveled to the famous club on St. Joseph Island.

That spring the initial February opening was erased from the public record. Always the promoter, Green announced that President McKinley would participate in the official Tarpon Club opening ceremonies, now slated for May 1. As intended, the news made national headlines. Green himself seemed to get caught up in the euphoria, excitedly pronouncing his intentions to construct a lavish new hotel in Rockport.

Green's Rockport hotel was a necessity, he said, because the Tarpon Club had been fully subscribed, its waiting list long. Planned for the Aransas Bay site that James Fulton initially offered Green for the club, it would be a three-story building with 100 rooms, all lit by electricity and heated by steam. Large turtle and fish pens would be "put into the bay, so that club members can always be supplied with something fresh." The undertaking was backed by investors promising $100,000 in capital for buildings, furnishings, and purchase of "steam pleasure boats." SAAP railway agent E.J. Martin, in a statement that likely raised eyebrows with his bosses, promised not to entertain travel arrangements with any other businessmen planning sporting clubs or hotels that might compete with Mr. Green's Rockport enterprise.

Plans for Green's Rockport hotel evaporated as quickly and quietly as President McKinley's aborted visit. The first of May was just another spring day when the much-heralded official Tarpon Club opening – in reality, its second or even its third – never came to pass.

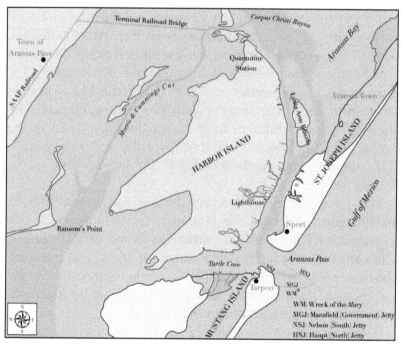

The Tarpon Club environs as they appeared between 1887 and 1900. Tarpon fishing and duck hunting was a significant contributor to Coastal Bend's economy. In just 13 years, the collection of small cottages at Ropesville grew into the town of Tarpon, the Tarpon Club was built with the hope that the town of Sport would grow around it, several jetty projects were attempted, the mainland town of Aransas Pass was founded along the track of the San Antonio & Aransas Pass Railway (SAAP), and the bridge from the mainland to Corpus Christi Bayou was rebuilt to handle trains. Illustration by R.K. Sawyer based on Robert Conley, "Sport Texas – A Luxurious Life, A Disinterested Death," *Journal of Texas Philately & Postal History*, Aug. 2021: 6-10.

Sam Gray's "elegant pleasure boat," the sloop *Aeneid*, hosted Green and company when they toured Mustang Island, initially surveying a site for the club location adjacent to the Seaside Hotel. It, along with Green's motor launch *Mabel*, later ferried guests to the Tarpon Club from Rockport. The *Aeneid* was a typical Gulf Coast scow with a wide beam and shallow draft, which enabled it to navigate the shallow waters of Coastal Bend. Collection of Jim Moloney.

The San Antonio & Aransas Pass Railroad (SAAP) connected San Antonio, Houston, and Waco to the Texas Gulf Coast. The SAAP was the main transportation artery for mainland Tarpon Club members and guests, who disembarked at Rockport before sailing for the Tarpon Club. The trip was slow by today's standards, taking some 14 hours to get from San Antonio to Rockport. Collection of Jim Moloney.

59

The only known image of Green's personal yacht, the *Mabel. Mabel* was launched behind Harbor Island on Nov. 16, 1898. It was the first gasoline-fueled vessel in Texas, the concept so novel that its captain, J. Ed Cotter, was sent to Chicago to "learn about the combustion and ignition of gasoline engines." Only insiders knew the origin of the name, Green's consort and future wife, Mabel Harlow. Note the town of Rockport in the background. Collection of Jim Moloney.

Architect's rendering of the Tarpon Club building (top) and the finished product (bottom). The structure was two stories high, shaped like a reversed letter 'L', and was 175 ft. long on the stem of the 'L' by 154 ft. 6 in. on the base line. The building was constructed entirely of wood and covered over 12,000 ft^2 of ground. Total floor area, including the tower, was 24,477 ft^2. With only 18 sleeping quarters, members and their guests were often quartered across the pass at the Seaside Hotel. Frank Hetfield in 1899 even renamed the Seaside the Tarpon Club Annex before redubbing it the Tarpon Inn a year later. Collection of Jim Moloney.

61

Club member C.W. Dawley's 7 ft. 10.5 in. tarpon, that weighed in at 175 lbs. Dawley caught the fish in 1899, the largest landed from a total of 444 tarpon that club members caught that year. It was prominently displayed at the Tarpon Club before it was later moved to the Bayside Inn at Rockport. Note that the postcard reproduced above shows a weight of 230 lb. for the fish. That weight is probably more correct than the 175 lbs., based on the size of the fish. Collection of Jim Moloney.

CHAPTER 6

OPERATING THE TARPON CLUB

The Tarpon Club was at the end of the world "and then a boat ride." Travelers first had to reach San Antonio, then relied on the SAAP Railway to deliver them, in relative comfort, as far as Rockport harbor before an eight-mile trip across Aransas Bay to St. Joseph Island. Although dozens of vessels were engaged to convey guests to the Tarpon Club pier, most of the traffic was handled by W.Y. Sedam of the *Lady Gay*, Captain Sam Gray's *Aeneid* that also conducted the mail, passenger, and express service, and Green's naphtha launch, the *Mabel*.

Another important part of the Tarpon Club's maritime operation was the transport of America's most distinguished citizens to and from the shooting and fishing grounds. In the era of sail and primitive gasoline engines, before modern communication and sophisticated weather forecasting capabilities, there was a lot that could go wrong.

Lifesavers. Coastal disaster response during the early 1800s was at first the responsibility of volunteers, mostly watermen who braved winter gales and summer hurricanes to rescue shipwrecked seamen using surf boats, hawsers fired from a Lyle gun, and breeches buoys. Rescue station operations were funded by Congress in 1848 and organized into the US Lifesaving Service in 1878. That year a lifesaving operation was established on the northern tip of Mustang Island, manned by local bar pilot John G. Mercer. In 1898, The year the Tarpon Club was built, the lifesaving station was under Keeper Edward White.

E.H.R. Green lobbied his Washington political cronies to relocate the original Mustang Island lifesaving station to St. Joseph Island. The move was warranted, he reasoned, because large numbers "of fine yachts" converging on his newfound maritime playground would be subject to "nautical perils" and potential accidents at sea. But the fine yachts of the millionaires never fully materialized, and the lifesaving station remained across the pass.

Weather Forecasting. Early storm prediction was a mix of folklore and observation, and every mariner had his own recipe. Its main ingredients were the presence and movement of cirrus, alto-stratus, and cumulus clouds, plus the direction, height, and frequency of Gulf swells, and the wind direction and intensity. The only instrument in their brew was a barometer, and they watched not only its absolute value, but the rate of change and the gradient difference between locations. A telltale sign of a major storm, they knew, was when the "quicksilver disappeared in the tube of barometer."

Confirmation of a potentially dangerous storm at sea was communicated by ships making port at Aransas Pass. The lifesaving station then dropped its regular flags, raising in their place a red flag with a black rectangular center signifying a major storm. The news at last reached the Corpus Christi weather station by boat.

Weather reporting in the mid 19th century was assigned to the Smithsonian Institution with a network of volunteers who telegraphed daily meteorological conditions to the Washington office. In 1870, Congress founded the US Weather Bureau as part of the Army Signal Service. Still relying on volunteers, the agency authorized the Corpus Christi weather station in February 1887. It was a major breakthrough when Captain H. B. Jackson of the Royal Navy's Torpedo School and Guglielmo Marconi developed wireless ship-to-shore communication in 1897. The town of Tarpon, however, did not benefit from wireless technology – the Mustang Island Lifesaving Service lacked both sophisticated radio equipment and a telegraph wire to the mainland.

64

Political cards were again dealt in the nation's capital when Green petitioned the Weather Bureau to approve a weather signal service office at the Tarpon Club. Green designed a weather room with the most modern "wireless telegraphy paraphernalia" and a new-fangled telephone line strung between the clubhouse and mainland. Whenever Green was at his club, he could be seen listening and tapping out messages late into the night from the cupola at the top of his building.

A New Postmark. Green wrote US Postmaster General C.E. Smith in Washington with yet another request – approval for a post office at the Tarpon Club. Smith certainly wanted to oblige him, but he wrote that his hands were tied – regulations stipulated that he could only authorize a post office in an established town or city. Green overcame the hurdle by naming his one-building clubhouse the town of Sport, Texas.

The Sport post office was established in 1899, its first postmaster 23-year-old Michigan native and former Dallas bartender, Carroll R. Evans, who doubled as a hotel clerk. A.R.A. Brice took over as the Sport postmaster in early 1901, also doing double duty as the Tarpon Club's "hotel keeper." Newspapers and letters did find their way to and from Sport, but mostly the office was kept busy with gourmet foods, fine liquors, and wine sent south from across the United States.

Working at Sport, Texas. The Tarpon Club staff lived both in Tarpon, across the pass, and at the clubhouse in Sport, their numbers varying seasonally. In the 1900 federal census, 27 people were listed as Sport residents. At the head of the list was Edward H.R. Green, a native of England whose occupation was listed as railroad president. Four families were living in the town: those of electrician Louis F. Bailey; 40-year-old hotel keeper A.R.A. "Robert" Brice, 36-year-old sailor Andrew Sorenson, and servant Laura Griffen. Seven others were listed as servants, both male and female, hailing from Texas, Mexico, and Virginia.

One of the more challenging tasks for hotel keepers Evans and Brice was managing visitor logistics. With only 18 sleeping quarters, members and their guests were often quartered across the pass at the Seaside Hotel. In a nod to the arrangement, Frank Hetfield in 1899 renamed the Seaside the Tarpon Club Annex before redubbing it the Tarpon Inn. It was a challenge for the hotel keepers to arrange boat traffic for guests strung between two locations with a channel between them. It was equally difficult to plan their sporting activities – some wanted to hunt, others to fish, and just as many were never able to make up their minds.

Far removed from Coastal Bend's supply and transportation infrastructure, the clubhouse staff not only had to expand their range of responsibilities, they had to be largely self-sufficient. The need for electrical, plumbing, and building maintenance and repairs was constant. Linens and laundry, cooking utensils, China, crystal, brass fixtures, and silver dining accouterments had to be either washed or polished by hand. After a hard blow, it could take a half-day just to sweep the sand from the first floor, and that didn't include the fine layer of silt that settled on all the furnishings.

Guests at the magnificent club building on the bay expected an attentive indoor staff to fulfill their every whim, and that responsibility fell to the wait staff – the "servants" – and the kitchen help. The kitchen was always open, and always bustling with activity. Beef, pork, fruit, and vegetables were shipped from the mainland, but everything else was harvested locally. Its menu was intended to serve the "educated palate" from a list that included diamondback terrapin, green sea turtle, shrimp, oysters, blue crab, fish such as red snapper, sheepshead, black bass, trout, flounder, redfish, and mackerel. In winter, plates were heaped with cranes, geese, ducks, a plethora of delicate shorebirds, wild turkey, quail, and venison.

The Life Saving Station (top) and crew (bottom) at Tarpon, Texas.
Collection of Jim Moloney.

E.H.R. Green lobbied Washington to relocate the original Mustang Island lifesaving station to St. Joseph Island because of the anticipated large numbers "of fine yachts" converging on his newfound maritime playground. Most likely the number of "millionaire yachts" that made sailed or steamed their way to the Tarpon Club was less than expected. Records from those that did make the journey are unavailable, except for a single photograph taken in 1900 by Bud West showing the private yacht *Prairie* that sailed to the Tarpon Club during its second year of operation. Nothing is known of its owner. Collection of Jim Moloney.

A letter sent from the Tarpon Club and postmarked Sport, Texas, March 19, 1900. Collection of Jim Moloney.

The mail boat from Rockport approaches the Tarpon Club pier in 1900. Mail was transported to Rockport via the San Antonio & Aransas Pass railroad then delivered on the mailboat to the Tarpon Club at Sport, Texas. Mail service was usually contracted to Captain W.Y. Sedam and his *Lady Gay* sailboat. Note the Aransas Pass lighthouse in the distance to the left of the boat. Collection of Jim Moloney.

The Tarpon Inn at Tarpon was originally named the Seaside Hotel when it was built in 1886. Anticipating more guests than the 18-bedroom Tarpon Club could handle, Frank Hetfield renamed it the Tarpon Club Annex in 1898 and by 1900 it was redubbed the Tarpon Inn, the name remaining unchanged for the past 122 years. Unlike the Tarpon Club's short reign of no more than six years, the Tarpon Inn has been a Mustang Island fixture for nearly 140 years. The building in this image was heavily damaged by the 1919 hurricane and replaced with the current structure in 1925. Collection of Jim Moloney.

A view of the Tarpon Clubhouse and pier from the Aransas Pass channel, showing both wings of the clubhouse. E.H.R. Green's weather room was in the high middle cupola and constructed with the most modern "wireless telegraphy paraphernalia" and a new-fangled telephone line strung between the clubhouse and mainland. One of the hotel keeper's jobs was to ensure sufficient supplies were on hand, as every item needed to sustain club members and their guests had to brought from the mainland. The only exception were foods that could be harvested locally, such as fish, fowl, turtles, oysters, and shrimp. Collection of Jim Moloney.

The dock at the Tarpon Club was the center of maritime activity. It was the
place visitors disembarked, supplies were landed, and the mailboat moored.
Guides, whether fishing or hunting, also came and went from the Tarpon
Club's long, wide pier. E.H.R. Green later added a large aquarium filled with
fish from local waters. Collection of Jim Moloney.

No details were missed at the elegant Tarpon Club, including a table set with the club's name monogrammed on its accoutrements such as this creamer and sugar. This set is one of the few artifacts remaining from the club, and is on display at the Port Aransas Preservation and Historical Association.

The Tarpon Club building was on pilings and the lower level open to the prevailing Gulf breeze. The 6,000 plus Hereford herd of Richard H. Wood and his sons roamed freely on the island. Most of the cattle were drowned during the hurricane of 1919. After the storm, a dead bull was found washed into the lobby of the Corpus Christi Nueces Hotel. Although over 20 miles to the southwest, it carried the Wood's signature St. Joseph Island "26" brand. Collection of Jim Moloney.

CHAPTER 7

BELONGING TO THE TARPON CLUB

The Tarpon Club was incorporated in 1898. Its original board of directors included Green, who advertised himself not as the president of the Texas Midland Railroad, but as the chairman of the Texas Republican Executive Committee; St. Louis banker J.C. Van Blarcom; former Texas senator A.W. Houston of San Antonio; former Dallas mayor W.C. Connor; and US Senator Matt S. Quay. Soon after its incorporation, the board's composition changed. Most notable in their absence were politicians Quay and Houston, although the latter remained a club member. Their roles were filled by Dallas businessmen John M. Simpson, Henry E. Hamilton, and E.M. Reardon.

One of the main duties of the 1898 board of directors was filling the membership roster, the names selected by invitation and from more than 1,000 applications received that year. Green personally signed each letter of notification for those admitted to the club.

When the member's names were announced, the press grabbed the story. Their reporting was rarely accurate, but nearly always sensational. In some instances, the lack of exactness was justifiable. Members died. Others were honorary memberships. But in most instances, the inaccuracies were leaked for publicity, and usually by Green himself. Green was an expert publicist and showman who likely refined the craft through counsel from another expert showman, his friend John Ringling of Ringling Brothers circus fame.

Under the headline "Playground of the first 400 Sportsmen of America," the *Dallas Morning News* on January 11, 1899, announced an unparalleled roster that included President William McKinley, former president Grover Cleveland, Pennsylvania senator Mathew S. Quay, Ohio senator Mark A. Hanna, and others of equal distinction. The *Houston Daily Post* thought it had an inside scoop when it announced members Charles A. Culberson and Joseph D. Sayers, the previous and newly elected governors of Texas, respectively. None of these men were, or would ever be, Tarpon Club members. But for ringmaster Green, what mattered was the perception.

Club Membership. The 1899 membership roster (APPENDIX 1) had 334 listed names. Over 200 were from Texas; 49 came from Illinois; and 43 from Missouri, of which all but one called St. Louis home. Another 29 were from Colorado, mostly Denver. New York was represented by 14 members, Illinois eight, five were from Ohio, and two from Pennsylvania and Arkansas. There was one member each from Massachusetts, Minnesota, Wisconsin, Kansas, Washington D.C., Maryland, Georgia, and the "Indian Territory." The only member not from the continental US came from Ontario.

The occupations of the men of the Tarpon Club reflected the leading businesses of the age – attorneys and judges, bankers, physicians and surgeons, railroad men, capitalists, and those with ties to insurance, real estate, oil, steel, manufacturing, mining, and newspapers. Politicians included past, present, or future senators, governors, and mayors.

Some of the names were well known in national circles. They included New Yorker Edwin Gould, heir to the Jay Gould estate; Isaac Ellwood of American Steel and Wire; and John Warne Gates of steel, oil, and railroad fortune. It is not known if Hetty Green ever knew that her nemesis, railroad baron C.P. Huntington, was a charter member of her son's club. He died in 1900.

The list of members who would have a political and business impact on Texas was also long. Among the better known were J.A. Baker, head of the Baker family legal dynasty; former Texas governor James S. Hogg; and Jesse H. Jones, a widely respected Houston banker and businessman who was later named chairman of Roosevelt's Reconstruction Finance Corporation. Also on the list were John G. Kenedy of the South Texas Kenedy Ranch and Robert J. Kleberg, lawyer and King Ranch manager, and the son-in-law of Henrietta King. Together they represented two of the largest ranch holdings in the American West.

About a dozen members of Green's state Republican party cronies were listed on the club roster. They included Thad C. Bell, J. H. Bell, G. G. Clifford, M. Dillon, William H. Gaston, John Grant, Henry Hamilton, O. S. Newell, J.C. O'Connor, Charles W. Ogden, and Edwin H. Terrell. Several were Republican candidates for the senate, such as E. C. Lasater and A.H. O'Neill. Club member George W. Brackenridge had been a Republican contender for governor in 1898, and G.W. Burkett was a 1900 Republican gubernatorial candidate. The editor of the *Burnet Bulletin*, convinced that Burkett would lose the race, wrote that the candidate, after his run, would quickly "sink back into oblivion." He did.

At least two Republican leaders on Green's roster were his political enemies. One was C.S. Cobb, leader of the Lily Whites faction who orchestrated the move to keep Green's name off the 1896 governor's ballot. The other was Cecil A. Lyon, another Lily White, who became Green's most bitter rival in the early 1900s.

Much of the Texas Midland Railroad brass were represented in the club, the list represented by treasurer Thomas E. Corley, who as a young man shared Green's Terrell bachelor quarters above the Harris Opera House; general counsel Charles W. Ogden; and directors T.W. House, J.S. Lockwood, and M.B. Lloyd, and agent J.E. Leith.

A Sporting Reputation. The business and political resume of the Tarpon Club roster is well documented in the public record. What is less known is the influence that many of these men had on the national and Texas sporting community. Many were either renowned outdoorsmen and early conservationists before their Tarpon Club tenure or earned their reputations later.

Club member William Northrup McMillan of St. Louis, heir to the American Car Foundry Co., was an explorer and African big game hunter. Among his accomplishments was a 1902 caravan expedition into the Sahara Desert, and in 1903 he sponsored a Nile River excursion of a thousand uncharted miles with an entourage of 100 camels, armed guards, and a flotilla of boats.

McMillan and his wife, Lucie, are also known for the 20,000-acre JuJa Ranch they leased from the British Crown near Nairobi, British East Africa. Credited with early studies of wild game animal behavior and domestication, some of the husband-and-wife team's groundbreaking findings attracted America's best-known zoologists and naturalists to their ranch.

Theodore Roosevelt, during an African expedition in which he harvested over 11,000 African specimens for the Smithsonian Institute's Natural History collection, was a guest at JuJa Ranch in 1909. To commemorate his visit, the McMillan's presented the former president with live African animals they donated to the National Zoological Park in Washington. An entourage of four lions, a leopard that had been Lucie's pet, two cheetahs, two gazelles, a warthog, and "a small vulture, a large eagle, and a large buto" were successfully transported by transatlantic steamer to the capital city, their journey supervised by a staff brought from the Smithsonian.

In another remarkable feat for the times, the McMillan's in 1910 presented five lions and a spotted leopard to the San Antonio Zoo. The animals, it was noted, were first "brought across the plains drawn by oxen" from their ranch to Nairobi, then shipped by rail to Port Said where they were loaded on an ocean-going steamer bound for Philadelphia. From there, they made a 1,700-mile journey to Texas by rail.

Chicago publisher and former Tarpon Club member William D. Boyce was another outdoorsman captivated by Africa. As a hunter, he had owned a sporting lodge in South Dakota, made forays across the Canadian territories from Hudson Bay to the Pacific Ocean, stalked big game in Mexico as a guest of President Diaz, and sponsored hunting safaris in Africa. Boyce was well acquainted with the Coastal Bend before he joined the Tarpon Club, spending several winters during the mid 1900s on Nueces Bay hunts with George Fulton and in Rockport with, as they were often known in the press, "the Bludworth boys" aboard their celebrated sailing scow *Novice*.

By the early 1900s, Boyce was intrigued by the growing theme of conservation, and in 1909 planned a mammoth excursion to chronicle the African landscape and its animals. Called the 'Blade's African Balloonograph Expedition' in a nod to Boyce's *Saturday Blade* newspaper, no one had attempted anything like it before. The images would feature moving pictures and "night flashlight views" collected from three balloons and "several small aeroplanes" along the trail of the recent Roosevelt Expedition.

The logistics were daunting. In addition to gear, supplies, and an entourage of 400 assistants, over 200 casks of sulfuric acid and stacks of iron casing were required to make hydrogen for the aeronautics. Together they filled 15 cars of the Uganda Railway then shuttled to a line of ox teams for travel to the border with German East Africa.

History mostly remembers the expedition as a failure. The lensman, writer, and project sponsor feuded. None of the telephoto lenses arrived. It rained for days. A lion chewed up a camera. There was either too much wind or not enough to launch the balloons, and one that did get airborne disappeared into the stratosphere, carrying with it a mule attached by a rope. Neither were ever seen again. When the expedition was alleged to have brought back more than 2,000 photographs of "wild animals in action and repose," some experts questioned if they were taken on the expedition at all.

Club member John Warne Gates was first known for his brand of barbed wire that stretched across the Texas range in the 1880s before creating a steel empire and discovering black gold at the famous Beaumont Spindletop oil field. In 1899, while he was a member of the Tarpon Club, Gates hunted waterfowl as the guest of railroad magnate Arthur Stilwell on the north shore of Sabine Lake. That morning they killed 900 ducks. Gates was so impressed with the hunt that he built a magnificent two-story colonial mansion on Sabine's Lakeshore Drive he referred to as his "hunting lodge." The city of Port Arthur grew up around it.

Gates's courted Tarpon Club member Isaac Ellwood – a sometimes adversary and sometimes business partner – at his Lost Lake Preserve. Guest Ellwood, like Gates, decided to spend part of each year in Port Arthur and in 1900 built the luxurious Pompeiian Villa on Lakeshore Drive as a hunting retreat. It stood in marked contrast to most hunting lodges, with a pink exterior and guest rooms that opened to a central veranda.

Tarpon Club member W.H. Patterson moved to Texas around 1900, establishing the Koon Kreek Klub in 1902. Located nine miles south of Athens in Henderson County, it was considered "the Mecca of Dallas sportsmen on the account of abundant fish and game." One hundred charter members paid $100 a share to purchase 7,000 acres and construct a half-mile long dam, a 700-acre lake, and a 19-room clubhouse. The club produced spectacular hunting. One Koon Kreek Klub member killed 365 ducks in a single day, and after daily bird limits were mandated in the early 1900s, Blind No. 9 on the main lake could produce up to eight limits of 25 ducks in a single morning. Member D.O. Mills killed three swans on one hunt.

A year after the Tarpon Club shuttered its doors, newspaper editor Frank P. Holland co-founded the Oak Shore Hunting Preserve, later renamed the Oak Shore Club. Located on the grounds of the Shell Hotel in Fulton, its membership was largely from Dallas and Ft. Worth. Oak Shore was known for its cuisine, its menu featuring venison, wild turkey, goose, duck, jack snipe, quail, fish, oysters, and even buffalo supplied by rancher Charles Goodnight.

Tarpon Club members and Texas railroad visionaries Samuel W. Fordyce, Jeff N. Miller and Richard J. Kleberg, the son of Tarpon Club member Robert Kleberg, completed the St. Louis, Brownsville, and Mexico Railway to the Rio Grande Valley in 1907. They opened several sporting hotels and clubs along its route. Railroad president Fordyce founded the Point Isabel Fishing and Hunting Club and built the nearby Beebe Hotel as a "hunter's paradise." Vice presidents Kleberg and Miller chartered the Point Isabel Tarpon and Fishing Club, and Miller opened the Jefferson Inn, built "especially for the sportsman." Club member Judge Wells, always the consummate host, welcomed orator and presidential candidate William Jennings Bryan for a duck hunt in 1911.

Before he joined the Tarpon Club, railroad man W.G. Crush made tarpon fishing and duck hunting trips to the Ropesville Seaside Hotel in the 1890s. An accomplished wing shooter, in the winter of 1894 Crush killed 160 snipes in three hours and 251 ducks in two days. He promoted Coastal Bend sporting clubs until his death.

Bryan Heard was one of the most medaled skeet and trap shooters in the state, competing with some of the nation's best shooters, such as Houston's C.L. Bering and Otto Sens. He later became president of the Texas State Sportsman's Association.

Tarpon Club members also had a significant influence on big game fishing. Member Alfred R. Whitney, from New York, was one of the nation's tarpon pioneers, making his first excursion to Florida in 1880. He fished Florida every year, covering the east coast from Indian River Inlet to the Keys, and on the west coast at Captiva Island. Whitney's record fish weighed 185 pounds.

Several Texans and future Tarpon Club members also fished Florida during the sport's formative years, notably San Antonio judge A.W. Houston and Texas senator P.J. Lewis. Both were considered among the most knowledgeable tarpon authorities in the United States during the late 1890s. It was Judge Houston, with his colleagues W.A. Adams, and W.P. Hardwick, who first discovered and promoted the tarpon fishing destination of Aransas Pass.

Houston's nickname for silver kings was 'Yucatan Traveler' because of their habit, after they were hooked, to head directly to South America. By 1905 he had landed more than 300. Judge Houston was a fishing companion to legendary naturalist and author Charles Frederic Holder, founder of the Tuna Club of Avalon on Santa Catalina Island. Dr. William A. Adams and

W.P. Hardwick should have had a lasting influence on the sport, but they died early. Hardwick was only 48 years old when, according to newspaper accounts, he succumbed in 1902 from a stomach hemorrhage "due in a measure to the shock occasioned by the death of Dr. Wm. A. Adams last Wednesday, the two having been very close friends of years' standing."

San Antonian J.S. Lockwood, a member of the Tarpon Club Board of Directors, was the first person in Texas to catch a tarpon over 100 pounds on rod and reel. His fish, landed at the Corpus Christi Bay shoreline of Flour Bluff in 1890, is what put Texas on the big game fishing map.

Houston angler Jesse H. Jones remained active in competitive tarpon fishing circles long after the club closed and is remembered as the sponsor of the Jesse H. Jones Loving Cup, the award presented to the angler who landed the most tarpon in any one day between 1910 and 1912. Jones, along with Judge Houston, were both members of the elite, 150-member Port Aransas Tarpon Club that was founded in 1907 by L.P. Streeter, Secretary of the Catalina Tuna Club. The club, headquartered at the Tarpon Inn, promulgated a "higher standard of sportsmanship" by encouraging the use of only light tackle and protection of big game fish species.

As for founder E.H.R. Green, after the Tarpon Club closed, he moved on to entirely different pursuits. He never again took an active part in wildlife, fisheries, or America's nascent conservation movement.

Tarpon Club member William Northrup McMillan, in later years, at the wharves on one of his many transatlantic voyages. McMillan his wife Lucie owned the famous JuJa Ranch in Africa. Theodore Roosevelt was among their many distinguished guests. Library of Congress, Prints & Photographs Division, LC-DIG-ggbain-18560, https://lccn.loc.gov/2014-698596.

A number of former Tarpon Club members continued to hunt and fish at Port Aransas after the club closed. One was San Antonio member George Eichlitz, shown here with Robert Ellington's Chesapeake Bay Retriever "Bill." Eichlitz was a regular client of Ellington, a former Tarpon Club guide, and his son Cyrus. Courtesy Bruce Baker.

Another former Tarpon Club member who founded a sporting club in Coastal Bend was newspaper editor Frank P. Holland (far right). A year after the Tarpon Club shuttered its doors, Holland co-founded the Oak Shore Hunting Preserve, later renamed the Oak Shore Club. Located on the grounds of the Shell Hotel in Fulton, its membership was largely from Dallas and Ft. Worth. The photo postcard was taken by Rockport photographer W.D.L. Dye in front of the Shell Hotel in 1913. Most of the harvest is made up of pintails and Canada geese. Collection of Jim Moloney.

CHAPTER 8

COASTAL BEND HUNTING

The Texas Coastal Bend couldn't have been more removed from the smoky boardrooms, political back rooms, and convention halls that ordinarily defined Green's haunts. High-speed trains may have already connected American largest cities, but only horses and wagons linked small Texas inland communities to the port towns of Rockport and Corpus Christi. While the waters surrounding Green's native New England were plied by fine yachts and steamships, Coastal Bend's maritime culture was, in contrast, centered around locally constructed wooden sailing craft, large and small. The financial district of Coastal Bend was comprised not of high-rise buildings like those of New York or Boston, but rather an amalgamation of boat captains running the back barrier island bays in pursuit of fish, oysters, and wild ducks they sold to fish and game merchants for distribution to America's seafood and wild game markets.

Waterfowl hunting was deeply imbued in the Coastal Bend culture, its origins dating back to at least the 1830s with the settlement of the first Europeans, mostly Irish, in the Power and Hewetson Colony of Mexican Texas. It was an easy, almost natural transition as, over time, the killing of waterfowl shifted from sustenance, then to market hunting, and finally to sport hunting.

Market Hunting. E.H.R. Green's Tarpon Club was founded during the last years of legalized market hunting in Texas, a time when the emerging conservation movement was beginning to focus its exertions on the carnage of the nation's wildlife by market gunners. Today it may be difficult to appreciate just how important the availability of wild game was to Americans, both to the everyday citizenry and on the tables of the continent's finest restaurants – where it was nothing short of a culinary phenomenon.

Demand for wild game during the 1800s to early 1900s was insatiable, but particularly for waterfowl, and it led to a major industry in killing, shipping, and handling wild birds. Canvasbacks, and to a lesser extent redheads, were valued by epicureans above all other wildfowl. The best canvasback ducking regions, the optimal diet of the white, black, and red diving duck, and preferred recipes for it were debated in newspapers, sporting journals, and in restaurant circles for at least a century. Because they commanded the highest market prices, canvasbacks and redheads were the chief prize for market gunners throughout the United States.

The Tarpon Club's hunting grounds were at the heart of Coastal Bend's most prolific market gunning region. Large numbers of canvasbacks and redheads wintered there each year, particularly in the waterways adjacent to Harbor Island. The economic opportunity attracted market men from Port Lavaca, Rockport, and as far south as Corpus Christi. During the late 1800s, Rockport alone was home to some 30 to 40 commercial gunners, its shipping merchants transporting approximately 75,000 ducks to northern cities each year during the 1890s, of which about 30,000 were canvasbacks.

Texas market men harvested wildfowl by whatever means they could, and it was business, not sport. Large birds, such as whooping cranes, sandhill cranes, swans, and geese were usually rifled or shot with scatterguns from horseback. Of the few records that remain from these largely unchronicled hunts, one was a three-day Coastal Bend shoot in 1894 in which brothers John Leonard and Thomas "Jed" Bludworth returned to Rockport with a rifled "white bugler crane" – local vernacular for the whooping crane – and 164 geese.

Smaller quarry, like ducks and shorebirds, were shot from blinds, or hides, by gunners using double barrel or repeating firearms. To maximize the volume of the kill they usually waited before taking the shot until a large number were grouped on the water. Blinds included rudimentary hides constructed from natural vegetation, pits dug on the shoreline, skiffs in shallow water, and in some instances, the infamous sink box.

Before they were outlawed, sink boxes were the most lethal blind used to harvest waterfowl. Popularized on Chesapeake Bay's Susquehanna Flats, sink boxes were a narrow, floating box in which the hunter lay prone at the water level and nearly invisible to decoying ducks. Exposed to the elements and at the whims of the seas, however, it was both a rigorous and often dangerous method of pursuit for both the hunter and the operators.

The earliest sink box operation in Coastal Bend was likely the single-man boxes constructed of galvanized iron by Louisiana-born ship's carpenter Bernard Leonard Bludworth during the mid-1890s. Sons John, George James (Jim) and Thomas (Jed) towed them behind their cat-rigged scow *Novice* for use in the family's market hunting business, and at times for the more stoic of their sport hunting customers.

Another commercial Harbor Island sink box operation was probably the largest of its type on the Texas Gulf Coast. The venture involved a small fleet of sloops, scows, and schooners with water-tight sink boxes that were two-feet wide, six-feet long, one-foot deep, and flanked by 16-foot sideboards. The crew rose each day before dawn to set the shooting box and huge decoy spreads before rowing hunters, packed with 500 to 1,000 rounds of ammunition each, to the line of boxes. A cat-rigged sloop tacked downwind to retrieve downed birds. Each schooner was filled with over a half-ton of ice to preserve the kill, allowing the gunners to remain on the shooting grounds for several days before shipping the birds to market.

Market men also hunted at night. The traditional method consisted of a lantern mounted on the bow of a rowing skiff, also called a sculling or punting skiff. The quiet of a Tarpon Club night was often pierced by the roar of repeating shotguns, eight- to four-gauge single or double bore swivel guns, or the

89

most infamous weapon of the time, the punt gun. Punt guns were six to nine feet in length with magazines that could hold up to a pound of powder and two pounds of shot to the charge. Weighing from 50 to 200 pounds, the big guns were rested on chocks with their large barrels pointed over the bow of the skiff. A single discharge by a gunner who drifted or paddled quietly into resting flocks sometimes left up to a hundred birds belly up on the water.

Sport Hunting. The sport hunter's tenure afield paralleled market gunners throughout the 1870s and early 1900s. They were very different kinds of hunters. Most sportsmen were urban and wealthy, their station in life allowing them the luxury of hunting wild game for sport, not to earn a living. Their guides were often former market gunners, many of whom had abandoned its rigors for the comparative comfort of bringing sport hunters safely to and from their hunting destinations.

Before the San Antonio & Aransas Pass Railway (SAAP) came to town, Coastal Bend's hard-scrabble watermen had never considered nature's bounty of fish and waterfowl as anything other than a commodity. The flow of people now heading south brought a welcomed measure of prosperity. They were willing to pay for a guide – and pay them well – for the opportunity to shoot ducks on the wing and pursue a single fish species with no commercial market value. The Coastal Bend sporting industry was born.

When E.H.R. Green selected Rockport as his mainland headquarters, its sport hunting and fishing infrastructure was already well established. In addition to its San Antonio connection via the SAAP railroad, the town had two hotels, the Congdon and the Bay Side Inn, that catered to visiting hunters and fishermen. When the Shell Hotel opened in the 1880s, northern sportsmen often booked its every room.

Coastal Bend waterfowl guides in the late 1800s to early 1900s were not just hunters, they were sea captains – skilled mariners who either owned their vessels or had charge of vessels belonging to wealthy syndicates. Their clients usually booked trips for several days to even weeks afield in a bay-worthy sailing craft, their draft deep enough to navigate open water. Their design, however, restricted shallow water access, so the ship's crew had to transfer guns, cases of ammunition, and hunters into smaller sailing tenders or pulling skiffs. Then helpers rowed to the hunting grounds, cutting brush to construct a crude blind, and setting dozens of wooden decoys.

Coastal Bend guides delivered some impressive hunts. One party killed 700 ducks, mostly canvasbacks and redheads, on a three-day shoot. Another shot 1,100 ducks in a day and 1,500 the following morning. Kansas City sportsmen on a St. Joseph Island trip in 1893 shot 84 canvasbacks along with geese, curlews, and swans. An Austin businessman who chartered William Armstrong's *Alice* for a week in 1899 returned with nearly 800 canvasbacks and redheads. San Antonio sportsmen on a hunt with Captain W.Y. Sedam of the sloop *Lady Gay* killed 450 ducks, mostly pintails, and redheads. A party of Ohio and Chicago politicians in 1899 wrote that "our party, in three days, killed over 500 [ducks]. It was not a remarkable killing when you consider the great number that came in at that time."

Only a few of the Coastal Bend boat captains worked exclusively for any one of the area's sporting operations. Most of them guided sporting excursions arranged by Corpus Christi and Rockport hotels, the Seaside Hotel (later the Tarpon Inn) on Mustang Island, and E.H.R. Green's Tarpon Club on St. Joseph Island. Even after telegraph wires connected the barrier islands to the mainland, hotels and clubs continued the tradition of hoisting a colored flag that broadcasted the need for a hunting guide.

Tarpon Club Guides. Some of the names of the Tarpon Club hunting guides include William Armstrong and his schooner *Alice*; W.Y. Sedam of the *Lady Gay*; Captain C.L. Dean, who had charge of the schooner *Oriole*; and Isaac Johnson, the original owner of the sloop *Aeneid*. Although no records confirm Denmark native Andrew Sorenson was a Tarpon Club guide, it seems likely.

Born in 1857, William Armstrong plied waterways from Corpus Christi to Espiritu Santo Bays for his entire life. Sailing his schooner *Alice*, named for his daughter, he first worked as a market hunter then later for the Texas Fish and Oyster Commission, earning a $150 annual salary overseeing oyster harvests. Armstrong was famously known for guiding writer William B. Leffingwell, whose 1888 publication 'Wild Fowl Shooting' was a classic among sportsmen. Armstrong made one of his last hunts in 1915, two years before he died, with his sons Clyde and Clarence. Their Kansas City Southern Railway customers returned to their private car with 600 ducks.

Captain W.Y. Sedam, who lived in Rockport, was not mentioned in the press as often for waterfowl hunting exploits as he was for catching sharks, both with a harpoon and later with rod and reel. Guide C.L. Dean, legend has it, was "the first actual settler" in Rockport, probably arriving in the early 1860s. In the years before the Tarpon Club opened, he had charge of San Antonio's George W. Brackenridge's schooner *Oriole*. One of Brackenridge's guests was Texas Governor Hogg, and both were founding Tarpon Club members. Ropesville's Captain Isaac 'Ike' Johnson was an early tarpon fishing and waterfowl guide, who – unique in Texas for the times – bred and hunted over Chesapeake Bay Retrievers.

Andrew Sorenson was one of the best-known sporting names in Coastal Bend. He lived for at least some time at Sport, modestly listing his occupation as 'sailor' in the 1900 Federal Census. His resume should have been much longer. By 1900, Sorenson had worked as a Coleman Fulton Pasture Company cattleman, waterfowl hunting guide, and was the proprietor of Sorenson's Camp at Swan Lake on Copano Bay, a popular destination for early Texas sportsmen. References to Sorenson's Camp include an 1895 hunting trip by San Antonio's Oscar Guessaz with a syndicate of Memphis capitalists who traveled in a private SAAP Pullman car, complete with a French cook who served a banquet that included Swan Lake canvasbacks.

After the Tarpon Club closed, Sorenson founded the Port Bay Club near Rockport on Copano Bay. It is probably no coincidence that its organization was very similar to Green's

Tarpon Club. In its first year the Port Bay Club sold shares at $150 each to 100 members from Texas, New York, Chicago, St. Louis, Cincinnati, Atlanta, Wisconsin, and Massachusetts. Almost immediately, trips to the club by persons of note from across the U.S. and Texas, mostly Waco, Dallas, and San Antonio, were a regular feature of newspaper society pages.

Sorenson and his son James B. Sorenson later managed the Oak Shore Club's Shell Hotel at Fulton, which was co-founded by former Tarpon Club member Frank P. Holland. By the time Sorenson died, he added two more titles to his impressive resume – advisor to the Waco-based Texas Game Protective Association, and for 41 years he served in several capacities with the Texas Game, Fish, and Oyster Commission.

Tarpon Club Hunting. Waterfowl hunting at the Tarpon Club usually lived up to its glowing reports. In a *Dallas Morning News* account, the writer described how "in early winter, arrive clouds of [ducks]. The air is alive with them; their wings make a continuous hum." The writer described "wild geese of all kinds" but erroneously proclaimed there were over 30 different snipe species. There was only one. It didn't matter – Ned Green didn't value accuracy as much as the media attention. He got it.

Most of the waterfowl harvested by club members were redheads, bluebills, pintails, wigeons, canvasbacks, greenhead mallards, and black or summer mallards that are today called mottled ducks. Snow geese and Canada geese were common, and at times there were large numbers of trumpeter and whistling swans. White-fronted geese, sandhill cranes, and whooping cranes were also occasionally harvested. What they hunted, and where they hunted, depended on the time of year and the weather.

The center of the fowling operation was the Tarpon Club pier, where guides met their charges each morning and, less commonly, in the afternoon. The pier was usually a confusion of rowboats, cat-rigged yawls, and sailing scows and sloops at anchor nearby as guides hollered out the names of their party. Then they loaded gear, ammunition, decoys, and hunters into whatever vessel was assigned to their hunting location.

Most club hunts were made at nearby Harbor Island. Requiring only a short sail across the Lydia Ann channel, the logistics of the hunt were simple enough that most hunters were able to return to the Sport clubhouse in time for lunch. Proximity to the club did not mean they didn't kill birds. The skyline above Harbor Island's winding bayous and fringing mangroves could be animated with redheads, bluebills, pintails, and canvasbacks. According to historian Robin Doughty, so many ducks were killed at Harbor Island that "sharks congregated to feast on floating birds before they could be retrieved."

Guides always followed the birds, and they sometimes sailed north to the Rockport shoreline near Traylor Island or headed east across Aransas Bay to Copano or St. Charles Bay with the more enterprising of their hunters. Here, thick mats of shoal and widgeon grass attracted uncountable numbers of redheads, bluebills, pintails, and wigeons in flocks that could cover miles of the water surface.

Excursions further afield, to the backside of St. Joseph Island or past Cedar Bayou that separated it from Matagorda Island, required a commitment of several days. The coves, flats, and points that characterized the back barrier island shorelines produced stunning hunts, particularly for pintails – or sprigs as they were usually called – as well as Canada geese, snow geese, and sometimes swans, sandhills, or whooping cranes. Although these trips were time consuming because of the distances covered, the hunt required only a few dozen wooden decoys and a short row from the larger sailing craft.

In contrast, hunts into the island interior were logistically demanding, necessitating mules and wagons for what might be a long journey winding through cactus and sand. Wooden decoys were almost never used because of their weight – instead, guides staked out the first birds killed during the hunt. The numbers of birds secreted between the sand dunes in freshwater ponds was rarely as impressive as on the bays, but the variety was greater. Covered in smartweed and southern naiad, the isolated potholes were home to most of the teal, gadwalls, black mallards, and greenhead mallards club hunters killed. In addition to harvesting sometimes hundreds of ducks and geese, they often traversed the back dune scrub line to kill wild turkeys, quail, and bobcats.

If they tired of duck shooting, or wanted a more challenging wing shooting sport, Tarpon Club members turned to shorebirds. Shorebirds presented a fast-moving target that required superior marksmanship, and for those who were up to the task, or aspired to be, the back side of St. Joseph Island presented a perfect opportunity. Here, wing shooters were poled in shallow-draft boats to hunt bitterns, rails, and snipes, or they shot curlews, plovers, and yellowlegs on the Gulf side's sandy beach.

In the era before daily waterfowl bag limits, or for that matter any hunting regulations at all, it was perhaps a first when the Tarpon Club set its own duck hunting season, from October 1 to April 1. During those six months, hunters killed a remarkable number of birds. A newspaperman explained that the club's huge harvests were defensible, as "members of the club are not market gunners, they kill mercifully and scientifically." Not everyone believed the hyperbole that followed the monied sportsmen. One Harbor Island market hunter watched disdainfully as club members, "including a state senator," spent a calm, clear day firing high-powered automatic rifles into resting flocks on the bay, adding that the club hunters "picked up only the fat ducks. They left all the others to waste."

There is no indication that E.H.R. Green ever went on a Tarpon Club duck hunt. The only reference to a Green hunt was one from the comfort of the *Mabel* on a 1900 excursion to the Brazos Santiago Pass, on the South Texas coast. Green, who took a shot at a flock of roosting birds on the water from his saluting cannon mounted on the deck, had loaded the gun with two pounds of shot and a pound and a half of powder. He killed over 120 birds.

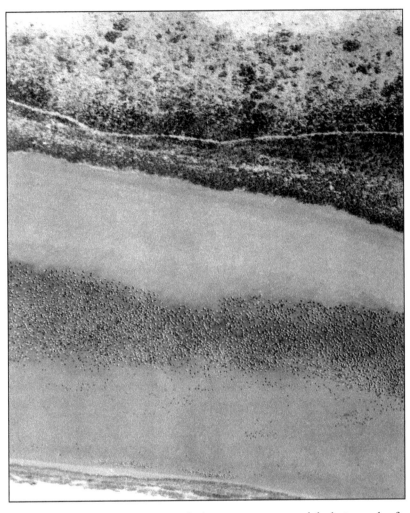

The way it once was. Too many ducks to count – an aerial photograph of pintails behind the barrier islands of the Coastal Bend. Courtesy Charles Stutzenbaker.

A typical scene after a morning hunt in the Coastal Bend of Texas. This photo postcard is from Tarpon, early 1900s, and shows hunters with a harvest of about 70 birds, mostly redheads, a few pintails, some bluebills and a canvasback or two.

There were no regulations governing migratory bird hunting during the Tarpon Club years. The first Texas game law was the Model Game Law, passed in 1903. In 1907, Texas approved the Permanent Game Law that included the first limit on the number of ducks that could be killed per day – a total of 25 – with a possession limit of 75. Senator Terrell introduced the 'Game Warden Act' that year that provided funding for a chief deputy commissioner and deputy commissioners, or game wardens, and the Fish and Oyster Commission was renamed the Texas Office of Game, Fish, and Oyster Commission (GFOC).

Rockport and the Coastal Bend played an important role in Texas conservation. The first GFOC commissioner was Richard H. Wood, one of the men who owned the St. Joseph Island land where the Tarpon Club was built. His son, William W., became GFOC commissioner in 1915. Several early game wardens were from the Coastal Bend. One was Captain William Armstrong, a respected Rockport sporting guide and former market hunter. Another was one-time Sport resident Andrew Sorenson, who served for 41 years in various capacities with the GFOC. Collection of Jim Moloney.

Ropesville's Captain Isaac 'Ike' Johnson shown with a litter of Chesapeake Bay Retrievers. Johnson was the original owner of the sloop *Aeneid*, and an early tarpon fishing and waterfowl guide. It was rare in the late 1800s and early 1900s for Texas hunters to use retrievers. Coastal Bend was evidently an exception, It is likely that the Chesapeake Bay Retrievers they used were brought by visiting northern hunters. Courtesy Port Aransas Museum.

This 1907 Rockport postcard shows a backdrop staged in the photographer's studio and is titled 'Two hours shooting' at Sorenson's Lodge. Andrew 'Pop' Sorenson (center) first guided hunters in the 1890s from his Sorenson's Camp, later Sorenson's Lodge, at Clubhouse Point on Copano Bay. He lived in Sport for at least the year 1900, where he listed his occupation as sailor. Sorenson is best known as the founder of the Port Bay Club, the oldest continuously operating hunting and fishing club in Texas. He also served for 41 years in various capacities with the Texas Game, Fish, and Oyster Commission.

The smooth-bore guns on the left and right are double-barreled side-by-sides with internal firing pins that were still common in the early 1900s. Repeating firearms such as the pump gun and auto-loader were becoming increasingly popular, particularly the 1897 Winchester pump (center) with its external hammer. The harvest is typical for Coastal Bend, consisting of mostly pintails, redheads, and a few mallards. Collection of Jim Moloney.

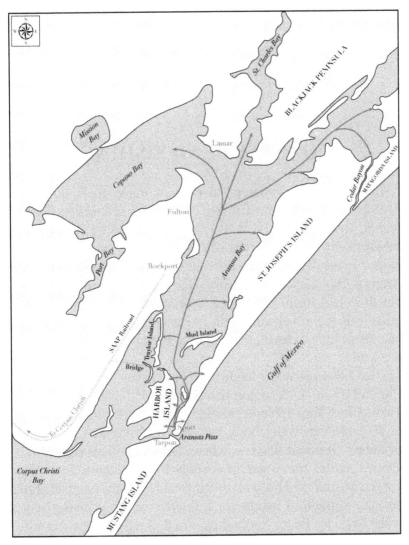

Guides transported their hunting guests throughout the Coastal Bend. Most Tarpon Club hunts were made on Harbor Island's bayous and fringing mangroves. Longer trips by sail from Sport took club members to Traylor Island, or they headed east across Aransas Bay to Copano or St. Charles Bay. Often several days afield were necessary for excursions to the back barrier of St. Joseph Island or to Matagorda Island. Less commonly, hunts were made to the island's interior isolated potholes. Wing shooters chasing bitterns, rails, and snipes, were poled in shallow-draft boats in the shallow marshes near the clubhouse. Illustration by R.K. Sawyer.

CHAPTER 9

COASTAL BEND FISHING

Aransas Bay commercial fishermen made their living by netting, using seines for fish and gill nets for sea turtles. During winter, most also harvested oysters by dragging iron-framed nets or hand-tonging. In the late 1880s, as the first tarpon were landed in western Florida, over 300 men were employed in the Aransas Bay fisheries industry. They were expert watermen, but they had little experience with sport fishing, particularly pursuit of the silver king with rod and reel. It not only didn't take them long to learn, they quickly became among the best in the world.

After J.S. Lockwood landed the first Texas tarpon at Corpus Christi Bay in 1890, tarpon fishing exploded in popularity. The Texas silver king epicenter shifted to the quarter-mile wide, 10- to 20-foot-deep water body between Mustang and St. Joseph Islands – Aransas Pass – where tarpon, it was discovered, danced across the water in schools by the hundreds as they gorged on mullet. The town of Ropesville and the Seaside Hotel became household names for followers of the growing sport, with Seaside Hotel proprietor Frank Hetfield the recently crowned king of Texas tarpon fishing.

An eager student, Hetfield kept meticulous records of what he learned by following the fishing news from Florida and from America's rod and reel nimrods who made increasing tarpon pilgrimages to Ropesville. Hetfield embraced parts of the Florida fishing model, most notably the use of small rowing skiffs manned by a guide, called a boatman, but soon introduced new methods better adapted to the area's waters. Under

Hetfield's leadership, Aransas Pass fishing improved each year. After every record from the previous four years was smashed in 1894 by H.M. Wallice, who landed five fish in a single day from a total of 48 strikes, Ropesville was renamed Tarpon in 1896 and Hetfield, capitalizing on his sporting success, changed the Seaside Hotel moniker to the Tarpon Club Annex in 1899. He soon changed it again to Tarpon Inn.

E.H.R. Green, who was a frequent visitor to the Seaside Hotel, quizzed Frank Hetfield relentlessly as he soaked up the subjects of tarpon and tarpon fishing. *Forest and Stream* listed the number of tarpon that Green's party landed on one of his last outings to the Seaside before he built his own club. Of those lucky enough to catch a fish, one was a guest by the name of Mabel Harlow.

Hetfield's new neighbor across the pass opened its doors for the 1899 tarpon season that, for consistent record-keeping, officially ran from April 1 to November 1. In its first year, Tarpon Club members and guests landed a total of 444 fish. The largest tarpon was caught by C.W. Dawley – at 175 pounds and measuring 7 feet 10.5 inches, it was mounted in the clubhouse. But it was Missourians J.C. Van Blarcom and J.W. Buck who dominated the fishing scene that year. Van Blarcom took the title for the largest fish taken on light tackle, a 5-foot-6-inch tarpon landed on "a No. 6 bass line, and a very light rod." He also caught the most fish, credited with 23 during the season in a tie with Denver's J.T. Mason. J.W. Buck came in second with a total of 22 fish for the season but held the record for landing seven fish in a single day.

In 1900, 63 club members and guests caught only 228 silver kings, about half the 1899 total. Van Blarcom and Buck no longer ruled the scoreboard, their season scores of five and three, respectively, paling to champion C.H. Booth's total of 15, which was four fish more than his closest competitor, Jack Gordon. That year Ned Green caught one. The dismal results of the 1900 season were largely due to the Galveston hurricane of September 8.

The Galveston storm was the worst natural disaster in United States history. Between its winds and storm surge, newspaper accounts reported that approximately 6,000 to 12,000 "persons passed from life to death during that dreadful night." The writers initially penned reports that Green was at the club during the tempest, his safety in doubt. Next came reports that the club buildings were heavily damaged. None of the reports were true. The town of Sport and the Coastal Bend were lucky.

Aransas Pass tarpon fishing hyperbola continued grow in the early 1900s, but its link to the Tarpon Club began to wane. After 1900 the Tarpon Club began combining their silver king numbers together with their neighbor, the Tarpon Inn, reporting it to the press as "the catch from Aransas Pass." Very little was mentioned about the club's 1901 fishing season, mainly that the first tarpon was caught on March 24, and that Tarpon Club fisherman J.T. Mason of Denver was in the record books again for landing 80 tarpon in less than a month.

Few Tarpon Club narratives appeared the following the year, either. That year, 1902, club fishermen averaged 12 tarpon a day, and the largest tarpon, at 6 foot 6 inches, was landed by Judge Houston's daughter. In 1903, published tales of Tarpon Club silver king exploits disappeared altogether.

During its short but regal reign, E.H.R. Green and the Tarpon Club set new standards in big game fishing. Green's club was among the pioneers in the use of light rods and tackle. Rather than baiting hooks with cut mullet, which was popularized in Florida, Green mandated that his boatmen use live bait. A fish hooked in the mouth had a better chance of surviving than one that swallowed the hook, he observed, and club members agreed it was more sportsman-like to battle a mouth-hooked fish. Other Green rules prohibited bringing any tarpon to gaff and to never kill a fish unless for mounting. As a result, boatmen rowed every sizable fish to shore, measured it, took off several souvenir scales, and returned it to the water.

Green kept copious notes on tarpon, his observations used by fisheries biologists to better understand their habits. Obsessed with the idea of being the first person to raise tarpon in captivity, he announced plans to erect "a mammoth tank" along the SAAP railway route to facilitate shipment, via a specially designed aquarium railroad car, of live specimens to the 1904 St. Louis World's Fair. In discussing the project, Green said "it may be possible, that by clipping off a section of the caudal fins we may keep one a prisoner, but I'll have to consult with the fish experts of the Government about it." Evidently the experts discounted the plan, as no live tarpons ever made their way to St. Louis.

Fish Stories. At its storied peak, accounts of the Tarpon Club's fishing feats were published widely, the tales eagerly penned by sportsmen and just as keenly consumed by the public. One writer depicted a day in which the pass was filled with dozens of small skiffs floating placidly with their lines out. In the distance, a black line propagated across the water surface created by a massive school of 'shiners' – as mullet were called – that was quickly followed by a frenzy of hundreds of rising tarpon. Boats here and there broke off from the flotilla with their fish. As the mullet and tarpon spread down the line, the silver kings were seen soaring several feet in the air and coming down among the bait, knocking them in every direction. Some leaped next to, others over, and some into the small skiffs. There were times when the pass was so alive with feeding tarpon that it was "dangerous to row a boat out among them."

On the clubhouse veranda or around the poker table, the most renowned big-game fishermen of the day debated such serious topics as the height a hooked tarpon could jump. One angler swore he saw "at least ten feet of blue sky between the fish and water," and had heard of a fish that vaulted entirely over the Aransas Pass rock jetties. Judge A.W. Houston recalled a tarpon that soared over his head and skiff and related the tale of another that "leaped over the rail and onto the deck of a Morgan Line steamer, which required it to attain a height of 15 to 18 feet." J.C. Van Blarcom added mathematics to his arguments, doing a triangulation exercise using distance and the height of his fishing rod to estimate the leap of one fish at 18 feet.

Tarpon weren't the only game in Aransas Pass and the Gulf. One guest caught 21 fish of six different species in a single day, his haul weighing over 350 pounds. Club members intent on big fish pursued swordfish, sawfish, manta rays they called the devilfish that could weigh nearly a ton, the calico ray "spotted like a tiger," jewfish, and sharks. Some used harpoons on the big fish while others pushed the limits of rod and reel. Captain W.Y. Sedam caught an 11-foot hammerhead in June 1898. The next year W.C. Connor hauled in a 300-pound black bass that he shipped on the SAAP to San Antonio. It fed the entire Rough Riders voluntary cavalry camped on the edge of town.

Tarpon Club Guides. In contrast to waterfowl hunting with its reliance on scow and schooner captains, the quest for tarpon was done mostly from small wooden rowboats. The men who had charge of the diminutive vessels were termed boatmen or pullers, and the best were in perpetual demand. Most of the Aransas Pass boatmen worked at both the Tarpon Inn and the Tarpon Club. A flag was raised whenever a puller was needed on either side of the pass.

Aransas Pass boatmen followed rules of the chase, an unwritten code of courtesies. Negligent was the boatman who failed to secure bait or load perfect equipment. They were never to anchor near another boat. If more than one angler was present when a fish was hooked, the other parties "should give the player the field" and reel in immediately. It was considered a "gross discourtesy" to cross another's line, and "criminal" to distract an angler who was playing a fish. If a large tarpon or other big fish threatened to overwhelm a single boatman, several others quickly roped their skiffs to his to prevent him from being towed to sea.

Boatmen during the tarpon heyday of the late 19th century earned their $2 a day salary. The job was demanding. Pullers rowed continuously for hours, trolling a live mullet with "some 300 feet of line being carried" and "kept near the surface of the water, not more than four feet below." This required that the boat be "in constant motion except when the tide is running strong," the job most challenging against an outgoing tide or while their charges fought a fish. The guides had to know exactly how fast to row, a delicate balance between a pace that would ease the strain on the line, keeping a hooked fish from breaking or stripping line, and getting the fish to tire.

The skiffs were small, the job at times dangerous. Large fish could crush the gunwales, and a puller's bones might be broken if a big fish leaped into the boat. As for gaffing a live fish, it was considered "a dangerous experiment to take a living tarpon into a light boat, as a lusty fish will wreck a skiff." If the fish didn't swamp them, storms and waves often did, particularly when they were dragged into the open Gulf by a large tarpon, shark, or manta ray. If a chain of boatmen couldn't stop the advance, the signal was given for the Aransas Lifesaving boat to come to their aid. Boatman Ed Cotter experienced the terror of being pulled into the Gulf and through the breakers many times, setting the unofficial record once when he came ashore several miles down the beach.

Customers marveled at the lean, bronzed boatmen of Aransas Pass. The best-known boatman at the Tarpon Club never apparently had a last name. He was known only as 'Ole Tony,' "the bent and grizzled Swede-Hungarian boatman" who was a fixture at the club. He had charge of the Tarpon Club boathouse, and for many years held the undisputed title as the champion 'puller' of Aransas Pass. Each spring Ole Tony kept his eyes cast to the sea, looking for the flash of silver among the schools of mullet that signaled the return of the tarpon.

Another of the better-known boatmen was Robert Ellington Farley, who settled in Ropesville in 1890 at the start of the tarpon craze. Farley was a taxidermist who mounted many of the area's tarpon, charging $12 for each fish. In 1902, his angler caught the world record jewfish on rod and reel, weighing in at a massive 450 pounds. Farley continued to guide fishing and hunting customers long after the Tarpon Club shuttered its doors. He was a self-made naturalist, and his knowledge of the outdoors later led him to curate the coastal Texas collection of mounted bird specimens and eggs for the Smithsonian Institute. Inspired by the decline in fish and game he witnessed during his years on the coast, he became a state game warden in the late 1920s.

J. Ed Cotter was a boatman at the Tarpon Club and later for his mother's Tarpon Inn. Another was an Italian immigrant named Mateo Brujen who was such a celebrated boatman that Charles Frederic Holder dubbed him the "Doctor of Tarpon." The name of Ed Kline, "a man of six feet and over, and of powerful build" emerges occasionally from dusty records, but little was recorded of his career as a boatman.

The Texas silver king epicenter was the quarter-mile wide, 10- to 20-foot-deep water body between Mustang and St. Joseph Islands – Aransas Pass. From the pass, the Tarpon Club appeared isolated from the world, an island oasis in a sea of saltwater. This is the scene that greeted visitors arriving from Rockport or returning from a day of fishing or hunting. The clubhouse was always a welcome and impressive site. Collection of Jim Moloney.

Tarpon Club members relied on local guides – the renowned Tarpon, Texas boatmen – to target the silver king. Boatmen rowed – or "pulled" – for hours, and it was demanding work. E.H.R. Green mandated that guides use only live bait to increase the chance of survival once a fish was returned to the sea. Note the Tarpon Clubhouse on the horizon. Collection of Jim Moloney.

Fishing the pass in 1900. The angler is identified only as Bud West, who may have been Tarpon Club member T.F. West. Collection of Jim Moloney.

The silver king was called the 'savanilla' or 'grand ecaille' in Texas before it became commonly known as the tarpon. When hooked, the "shimmering, silver-sided royalty" provided an exhibition of erupting water and aerial acrobatics. Collection of Jim Moloney.

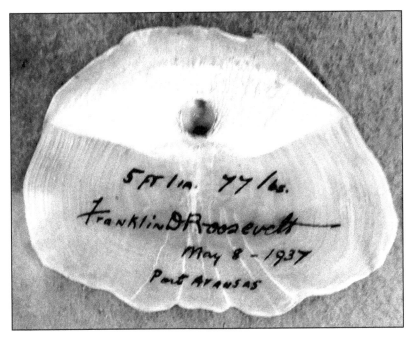

The tradition of releasing a landed fish became the mantra of all respectable tarpon anglers, who limited their bragging rights to a few of its metallic scales. The name of the fisherman and the fish's weight and length was carefully scribed. Often the scales could be over 4-in. in width. The Tarpon Club's scribed scales were once displayed at the Tarpon Inn but destroyed in the 1919 hurricane. The scale above is from President Franklin Roosevelt's tarpon fishing trip to Port Aransas in 1937, and is currently prominently displayed in the lobby of the Tarpon Inn at Port Aransas.

J. Ed Cotter (right), captain of E.H.R. Green's *Mabel* in a 1907 postcard. About this time, skippers like Cotter established the practice of towing the small skiffs to the channel to chase the silver king. The shores of Mustang Island and the Tarpon Inn are in the background. Collection of Jim Moloney.

CHAPTER 10

COASTAL BEND YACHT RACING

In addition to sport fishing, the Tarpon Club shared its summer season with another popular water sport, yacht racing. Coastal Bend racing was well established by the time E.H.R. Green arrived, and no one was surprised when he threw himself into the sport. His Tarpon Club sponsored the first summer sailing regatta in 1898, a year before the club even opened.

Coastal Bend was home to some of the Lone Star State's most trophied sailboat racers. The first races originated with the Rockport's Aransas Pass Yacht Club, founded in 1888. That year its organizers sponsored the Texas State Challenge Cup sailboat races, its prize a nearly two-foot, solid silver cup purchased for $500 from New York's Tiffany & Company.

To the Rockport helmsmen's chagrin, however, their costly cup was immediately nabbed by Galveston racers at the first Challenge Cup regatta. Certain of a second victory, the Oleander City sailors didn't bother to bring the trophy with them when they returned in 1889. But that year they were soundly thrashed by Rockport's Captain Sam B. Allyn in the cat sloop *Alice*. Confident that the loss was a fluke, the Galveston club decided to maintain possession of the coveted cup. A public scolding questioning their lack of sportsmanlike conduct and an appeal by a team of lawyers convinced them to secure its return.

Galveston racers entered an undefeated New York skipper with a northern-built boat to represent their city at the 1890 Rockport Challenge Cup. When they learned that the cup's defender was John Leonard Bludworth, an untried 23-year-old captain with a crew two younger brothers, they sensed an easy victory.

Bludworth family patriarch Bernard Leonard Bludworth moved from Louisiana to Matagorda before settling in Rockport, where he started a boat building business in 1880. When he wasn't crafting boats, Leonard supported the family through market hunting and commercial fishing. He passed his trades onto his sons, who evidently learned them very well.

The Bludworth family already had a reputation as Coastal Bend's most talented boat builders and sailors, having refined the design of their Gulf Coast scows – cat-rigged single masted sailing crafts ideally fitted for the shoal waters of Coastal Bend – to an art form. The Bludworth sons, however, were about to extend their reputation beyond local waters, and to an entirely loftier level.

Using mahogany driftwood hauled from St. Joseph Island, John, and his brother George James, known as Jimmie, designed and built a 31-foot cat-rigged centerboard boat with a 12-foot beam that, while it drew only 34-inches of water, was "still seaworthy in the open Gulf in all kinds of weather." When later asked to share his ship's plans, John admitted that he never drew it out. He just built it. In fact, he never put any of his boats to paper, then added "but I'm going to sometime."

Dubbed *The Novice of Rockport*, the underdogs of the 1890 Rockport regatta beat every Galveston contender and their New York entry that year. They went on to sweep the 1891 and 1892 Challenge Cup regattas as well. The Bludworth boys also competed in races in Louisiana and Mississippi, and from 1890 to 1892, they dominated the circuit.

The "famed flyers of Galveston," intent on knocking the *Novice* sailors from their pedestal, challenged the Bludworth's to a match in their own waters in 1892 at the Anheuser-Busch Challenge Cup. When John sent word he would accept their invitation only on the condition of a substantial prize purse, "a few gentlemen" organized a side race. Five-hundred dollars was quickly raised for the contest between the *Novice* and the pride of the Galveston fleet, the *Country Girl*.

The Bludworth boys grabbed the Galveston prize money. Rockport planned a grand celebration in honor of their achievement, but their designs were thwarted when the champions, sailing home after their triumph, arrived nearly a day early. The *Novice* had made the best time ever recorded between Galveston Bay and Rockport Harbor that day, and it wasn't even a race.

After the *Novice* won every contest between 1893 through 1896, the Galveston sailors surrendered. The city was unable to find a single enterprising yachtsman willing to compete against the Bludworth's at the 1897 Challenge Cup. Galveston wasn't alone. The Bludworth's had dominated large yacht racing for so long that no boats would go up against them. Their success posed a problem for the Rockport regatta organizers until they added a new boat category, the 20-foot class, to the racing docket. The smaller, more affordable boat was an immediate success, the 1897 race quickly filling with contestants from nearly every sailing town in Texas.

A festive atmosphere greeted Rockport visitors during the three-day Challenge Cup Regatta and "carnival of sports" in July 1897. The SAAP ran back-to-back excursions from San Antonio to deposit spectators, and boats sailed or steamed in from as far away as Sabine Lake to the east and Brownsville to the south. The schedule of events listed bicycle races, baseball tournaments, bands, balls, a "promenade concert," a litany of "theatrical attractions," and horse races that included a popular "West Texas broncos" entry. Although there were no challengers for the Bludworth boys and their *Novice*, both the "second-class" yacht series and the 20-foot class races were well attended.

The 1897 Challenge Cup Regatta caught the eye of E.H.R. Green. With its combination of outdoor sports, competition, and festival atmosphere, it was the kind of affair that always appealed to him. He told pressmen to expect "that the next regatta will be the best one ever had here." The next summer,

115

E.H.R. Green was the Rockport regatta's new sponsor, and the Challenge Cup trophy got a new name – the Tarpon Club's Cup.

If Green didn't deliver on his promise to make the 1898 regatta the most grandiose of the Rockport races, he certainly did in 1902. Promoter Green's regatta, timed with the grand opening of Rockport's new Del Mar Hotel, attracted over 700 visitors to the seaside resort. The SAAP's "special trains" arrived around the clock, the festival goers including Green's San Antonio entourage whose trip was reported under the newspaper headline "Millionaires Down at Green's Club House in Large Numbers." Master of ceremony Green was at his best, motoring from Sport to Rockport aboard the *Mabel* before joining the fleet to fire the starting cannon.

E.H.R. Green was not aboard his flagship *Mabel* at the 1903 regatta, the last year the Tarpon Club sponsored the event. It was also the final year of the Challenge Cup races and its Tarpon Club Cup trophy. As for the Bludworth boys, they had sold the *Novice* in 1902. Galveston area newspapers carried the news like they would an obituary, providing readers with a summary of its racing history, the respect it and its captains garnered among competitors, and ended the epithet with "she beat everything in her class."

The Bludworth's cat-rigged Gulf Coast scow *Novice* crossing the finish line of the 1893 Texas State Challenge Cup in Rockport. Challenging the *Novice* was the Galveston vessel *Wasp*, which lagged far behind. Using mahogany driftwood hauled from St. Joseph Island, John L., and his brother George James, known as Jimmie, designed and built the 31-foot cat-rigged centerboard *Novice* with a 12-foot beam, that drew only 34-inches of water. Its racing sails consisted of a mainsail, standing jib, balloon jib, and spinnaker. Note one of the "Bludworth boys" handling a fore sail on the bowsprit of the winning racer. The yacht *Cannie*, the first sailing craft family patriarch, B.L. Bludworth, constructed when he moved to Rockport, may be the boat marking the finish line on the left. Courtesy Texas Maritime Museum in Rockport.

TEXAS STATE CHALLENGE CUP.

THE TARPON CLUB'S CUP.
(From Photo by Randall.)

E.H.R. Green was the 1898 Rockport regatta's new sponsor, and the Challenge Cup trophy got a new name – the Tarpon Club's Cup. *Houston Daily Post*, Sept. 25, 1898.

The race for the Tarpon Club's Cup coincided with the opening of Rockport's Del Mar Hotel in 1902. The regatta drew over 700 people to the seaside resort with SAAP's "special trains" arriving around the clock. Top image from the *San Antonio Daily Light*, June 4, 1902, bottom image from Collection of Jim Moloney.

119

CHAPTER 11

ENDING THE TARPON CLUB

The Tarpon Club's future seemed uncertain almost as soon as it opened its doors, its tenure intertwined with and paralleling Green's political rise and fall. E.H.R. Green's impressive ascent in the state's Republican party began to unravel as early as 1898 when, during Green's Republican state chairmanship run, the Lily Whites, led largely by Congressman Robert B. Hawley of Galveston and Henry C. Ferguson of Fort Bend County – the Hawley faction, as it was called – nearly unseated him. Green persevered by only a narrow margin. More importantly, it showed the party he was vulnerable.

Two years later, the Hawley faction triumphed over Green for control of the Republic National Committee at its 1900 Philadelphia convention. He would have been just a footnote in Texas political history except for loyal friends in high places who pulled party machinery levers on his behalf. Citing a technicality based on "improper credentials," Green's network managed to overturn the entire slate of Hawley convention delegates that summer. The E.H.R. Green ticket was reinstated.

After his Philadelphia coup, the Republican Executive Committee met in several secret sessions to broker unity. Neither of the Texas sides would budge, and by the time the San Antonio convention opened in September at Beethoven Hall, the Hawley-Green supporters were about evenly matched. It promised to be a bitter political scrape. Green and his supporters opened by banning the Hawley contestants from the convention. Hawley raised the ante, renting the Grand Opera

House where he held a "bolting" convention in opposition to Green. The Texas Republican Party was hopelessly divided.

By October the Republican brass in Washington were reconsidering their Green support. Behind the curtain was Ohio political kingpin Mark A. Hanna who, as one of the most powerful backroom Republican politicians in the country, pulled most of the federal appointment and patronage strings. Determined to protect his recent victory, Green resorted to an unusual tactic – he persuaded former Democratic Texas governor and Tarpon Club member James Hogg to mediate with Hanna on his behalf. The substance of their discussion was never disclosed, but among political pundits, the move caused "considerable comment."

Governor Hogg's intervention had no impact. The Republican National Committee reversed their Philadelphia position, deciding in favor of the Hawley faction. Hanna tersely instructed Green and his supporters "to fall in line." In his concessionary telegram to Hanna, Green hadn't lost his wit. Your decision, he wrote, "reminds me of the wise remark which you recently made to me in Chicago – that you and I were fools to be in politics. You have been kind enough to help me out of politics, and whenever I can return the favor, please call on me." Hanna wasn't amused, his response curt: "I hope you will make every effort to reconcile differences between the Republicans of Texas."

Privately Green fumed, then publicly pronounced he would not seek reelection to the state chairmanship. At a press conference from the Menger Hotel, the deposed Green conceded to the Hawley contingency and their choice of Cecil Lyon as his state chairman replacement. The year was 1900, and it was only the second year the Tarpon Club was in operation. If the club was one of Green's tools for political gain, it was failing. Cecil Lyon was still listed as a member, but he made no appearances that year. Mark Hanna was no longer even rumored to be on Green's Tarpon Club roster.

By 1902, the press surrounding the Tarpon Club began to go silent. Trips by E.H.R. Green to Sport were less common, and when he did visit, he was usually accompanied by railroad or businessmen, not politicians. He had something of a political comeback that year when, with Hawley and Lyon, the three men took the podium together at the state convention in Fort Worth. The dueling politicians had negotiated an arrangement – Green would be the permanent Republican state chairman and conduct the Texas campaign, Hawley was named temporary state chair and head of the national committee, and Lyon was reelected state chairman. It was a remarkable show of unity, but it began to unravel almost immediately.

There may have been a hint that the fabled club was nearing the end of its short run that year when the *Houston Post*, in November, carried the announcement that the Seaside Hotel, in Corpus Christi, was changing hands. Its new manager, A.R.A. Brice, would operate it "in conjunction with the Tarpon Club."

Green did not publicly discuss the club in 1903, and he seemed to mostly avoid the place. So did the press. Newsmen from Galveston, Brownsville, and Houston rarely made mention of the Tarpon Club, penning little, if anything, about its hunting season or tarpon fishing, their coverage instead replaced by news on recently founded big game fishing clubs closer to their own shores. Only San Antonio, and to a lesser extent Dallas, featured short blurbs in their social sections on the comings and goings of club members.

It was the same with the national media. Once enamored by anything E.H.R. Green, scant mention was made of the Tarpon Club that year. The names of those who came for its opulence, or to rub shoulders with others of their economic stature, were for some reason no longer relevant. Or maybe they had just stopped coming.

With little fanfare, the doors of the Tarpon Club were closed by the spring of 1904. When a group of dignitaries traveled to Rockport to view work on the Aransas Pass jetties that year, the party was hosted on Green's yacht, the *Mabel*, but they lodged across the pass from Sport at the Cotter's Tarpon Inn. Green was not among the party.

Green was also conspicuous in his absence from state politics that year. The 1902 Green-Hawley-Lyon harmony proved to be fleeting, and now Hawley and Lyon had turned on each other. In his withdrawal announcement, Green said he had "retired from politics in disgust, finding it treacherous." That year, political kingmakers Mark Hanna and Mathew Quay died. Nothing in their obituaries mentioned their membership in the Tarpon Club.

Last Writes. In July, writer M.I. Lam sailed to the south end of St. Joseph Island on the schooner *Katie M.* from Corpus Christi. He was entirely unimpressed by what he saw. The legendary Tarpon Club clubhouse, Lam wrote, was little more than a "gigantic old wooden shell" located at a most "uninviting place." Lam went on to question why any sane person "would place their precious lives at the mercy of the treacherous waters of the Gulf at so dangerous a point." In this, he missed the point. In the gilded sporting era at the dawn of the 20th century, that was exactly the reason they came.

A.R.A. Brice, now the new manager of Corpus Christi's Seaside Hotel, peered out the train window. It was November 1904, and he was headed to Dallas to meet with E.H.R. Green. Retracing the part of the route between Rockport and San Antonio so often traveled by Tarpon Club sportsmen, he must have felt a little introspective. In his briefcase was a contract from Beaumont businessman J.J. Copley, the recent buyer of the 120-room Alta Vista Hotel near Corpus Christi, with an $8,000 offer for the Tarpon Club building, furnishings, and the *Mabel.* Copley had no intention of reopening the club. Instead, he would tear it down and use its pieces for the Alta Vista building. Green only glanced at the documents before hurriedly signing his name.

Captain Charles Wainwright was supervising the dismantling of the abandoned clubhouse during the winter of 1905. Workmen peeling back the layers of the club started with the furniture, then the hardware and electrical, and finally stripped the frame of its cypress and pine. As the parts of a once opulent sporting lifestyle were loaded onto a barge bound for Corpus

124

Christi, one of the workers removing furniture from the poker room found a roll of $600 hidden in a drawer. Its return to E.H.R. Green by the honorable workman was the last mention of the Tarpon Club in the press.

South Texas newspapers advertisements for Corpus Christi's Seaside Hotel were first published in May 1904. A.R.A. Brice, the hotel proprietor, was the former Tarpon Club manager. Collection of Jim Moloney.

GREEN'S FINE CLUB HOUSE

Has Been Purchased By J. J. Copley and Will Be Moved to Corpus Christi at Once.

On November 25, 1904, the *Corpus Christi Caller* reported:

J.J. Copley, a man of few words and, with an eye to business, purchased the celebrated club house on St. Joseph Island this week from E.H.R. Green, the sale being made through Mr. A.R.A. Brice, proprietor of the Seaside Hotel, who went to Dallas to see Mr. Green and close the sale to Mr. Copley. The purchase includes not only the fine club house and all its furnishings, electric light plant, etc., but also Mr. Green's fine launch the *Mabel*.

The fine club house, which was erected several years ago at a cost of $30,000, and which has been the resort of millionaires and noted sportsmen, was purchased at a bargain, as was also the launch, the entire amount being less than $8,000.

The club house will be taken down at once and moved to Corpus Christi and used in connection with the Alta Vista, which is to be opened as a grand seaside and tourist hotel on the cliffs south of this city next May...The *Mabel*, which will be brought here next week, will be run between Corpus Christi, the Alta Vista and other points on the bay.

126

The Alta Vista Hotel was located 3 miles south of Corpus Christi on the bluff overlooking Corpus Christi Bay. The Tarpon Club, dismantled after it was sold in late 1904, was used to complete the interior of the hotel as well as the wharf and outbuildings at the hotel. The Alta Vista opened in 1905 and closed after a few years. Collection of Jim Moloney.

After the Tarpon Club closed its doors, renowned big game fisherman L. P. Streeter founded another private fishing club in 1907 called the Port Aransas Tarpon Club. Its headquarters was the Tarpon Inn, and J. Ed Cotter was club secretary. Collection of Jim Moloney.

The empty sand beach once occupied by the Tarpon Club became the site of the Gulf Fisheries Company menhaden factory and wharf, which began operations on May 1, 1916, at approximately the same location as the Tarpon Club. It employed some 200 men to process catches of the large schools of menhaden found in the Coastal Bend. Like the Tarpon Club it was short-lived, victim to the hurricane of August 18, 1916, that demolished the plant just months after it was built. Collection of Jim Moloney.

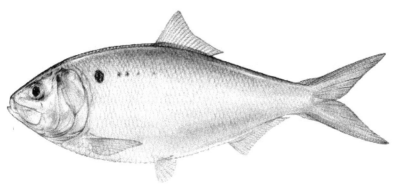

It is with some irony that pursuit of the legendary silver king on the shores of St. Joseph Island was replaced by the menhaden, a fish about 8 in. in length that seldom exceeds a pound or so in weight. It is an important Gulf Coast bait fish, but used only by humans for fish oil and meal for industrial/agricultural purposes. Menhaden are found in very large schools in the warmer inshore and near shore waters, following an annual coastal migration each year. Collection of Jim Moloney.

128

Today, the western shoreline of St. Joseph Island is probably similar to how it must have appeared to the first intrepid visitor, Spanish explorer Alonzo Álvarez de Pineda. Nothing remains of the Tarpon Club or the menhaden factory. The photograph above was taken in June 2022 at the former location of both structures.

Sam B. Allyn sold his St. Joseph Island interests to Richard H. Wood and his sons in the 1912. During the 1919 hurricane the Woods lost nearly 6,000 cattle, the financial loss contributing, in part, to their decision to sell St. Joseph to Cyrus B. Lucas in 1922. The island was purchased for $25,000 by Texas oilman Sid W. Richardson in 1936. Richardson built a private hunting lodge, designed by O'Neil Ford, to entertain friends, businessmen and politicians. After Richardson's death in 1959, the island was inherited by his nephew, Perry Bass. St. Joseph, renamed San Jose in 1973, remains the private property of the Bass family. Collection of Jim Moloney.

CHAPTER 12

LIFE AFTER THE TARPON CLUB

To follow E.H.R. Green is to follow a man of immense energy, talents, interests, achievements, and passions. His life resume looks as if it were compiled from more than a dozen men. By the time Green was 30 years old, he was president of a railroad and bank, politician, and had founded the nation's most extravagant sporting club. Before he left Texas in 1910, he added to the list several patents as an expert inventor, contributor to the costly boll weevil scourge, development of groundbreaking horticulture practices, and he was a key figure in the popularization of early automobile racing.

Even during the Tarpon Club years between 1899 and 1904, Green was a man with many interests and distractions. First and foremost was politics, and despite his litany of other accomplishments, his political ambitions would always elude him.

Politics, Again. Green's 1904 political retirement proved to be brief, reemerging at the head of the Black and Tan's in 1906 as part of an underdog move to capture the convention held that year in Houston. Calling themselves the "Reorganized Republicans," Green procured a supreme court order ensuring recognition of his new splinter group on the official ballot. When state chairman Alexander W. Acheson's gavel fell announcing the Reorganized Republicans nominee for governor, the choice of E.H.R. Green was met by wild cheering.

The bold move was doomed from the beginning. It wasn't just the Lily Whites who opposed the Green ticket – this time he had few allies in the press. One major newspaper penned that the turnout at the Reorganized Republicans' convention was mainly made up of "negroes," mostly "janitors, hack drivers, [and] chimney sweeps" who were prevented from working their "accustomed haunts" because of Green's political charade. There was no doubt that party leader Bill McDonald, another newspaperman mocked, had already set his sights on somebody's money, whether it was Green's bankroll or "superintending the federal patronage in Texas." Even Green supporters thought he was making a gross political miscalculation.

The Black and Tan Reorganized Republican convention drew only 200 delegates. On October 5, Green withdrew his nomination for governor. This time, E.H.R. Green was finished, and he was uncharacteristically silent about this final defeat.

In the end, the only legacy of his Reorganized Republicans was the colossal confusion they created on the ballot that year. County leaders received two slates of candidates, one from the Lyon-led sanctioned Republican party, and the other from the Reorganized Republicans. The result was bad for them both. Democrats seized the day, winning handily at nearly every level as well as the prized governorship. The Reorganized Republican candidate who replaced Green, A.W. Acheson, was barely a historical footnote.

Green's ties with the state Republican party were lastingly severed when he shifted his support from the Hawley-Lyon gubernatorial choice of J.O. Terrell in 1910 to Democratic candidate Oscar B. Colquitt. For his support, Colquitt offered Green a military advisor staff position that carried the title of lieutenant colonel. Green called himself 'Colonel' for the rest of his life.

The grand old party of Texas was in a shambles. The 167,000 votes garnered at the 1896 national convention under Green's leadership had dropped to an anemic 26,300 by 1910. Republicans from Austin and Travis counties continued to push for Green's return to politics, but he would have none of it. For most of 1911, he remained in New York, his absence the subject of much speculation. Former Tarpon Club member Cecil Lyon was still raking Green over the coals as late as 1912, putting the blame on him for the pathetic state of the party.

Inventor Green. Politics wasn't the only diversion that kept Green from the Tarpon Club. Another was Green's fascination with science and engineering. Inventor Green had a role in adapting electric headlights to use on locomotives as early as 1894, and six years later was the first to adopt high-speed hybrid gas-electric rail cars. He held patents on an electric gas lighter and a gas-burning signal lantern that were erected along his rail tracks.

The "railroad president-inventor's" grandest achievement, to that time, was the result of 1902 trip to Europe to study wireless telegraphy. Green wanted the TMR to be the world's first railroad connected by wireless communication, and back in his Terrell workshop, he designed a system that could be installed on moving trains. Consisting of two receiver sets fitted in his baggage cars and a transmitter in Terrell, he was awarded a patent for the invention, although the powerful "Marconi syndicate" – the Marconi Wireless Telegraph Co. – prevented him from ever capitalizing on it.

The Automobile. The ink was hardly dry on the Tarpon Club by-laws when Green was sidetracked by another interest. He had correctly anticipated that another newfangled invention – the automobile – would alter America's future. Although the horseless carriage would come to largely replace railroads – eventually including his TMR – Green embraced it, and is crediting for bringing the first gasoline-fired automobile to Texas. Shipped from St. Louis in October 1899, engineer George Dorris and co-pilot Green drove the 30-mile distance from the Terrell depot to Dallas in the remarkable time of just under six hours.

Green had a second vehicle delivered in 1902, one that garnered much attention for driver Jesse Illingsworth and passenger Green on its route to Dallas. Green said of the drive: "It was amusing to notice the sensation caused along the road. Cotton pickers dropped their sacks and ran wildly to the fences to see the strange sight. One razorback sow that caught sight of us is running yet, I know. At least a dozen horses executed fancy waltz steps as we sped by, and but for the fact that we were so soon out of sight, there would have been several first-class runaways."

There were. Although two attendants walked in front of the machine to clear livestock and horses from the track, it wasn't enough. Green and his driver, who hurled into Dallas at a "reckless speed of 12-mph" infamously left "a trail of wreckage and damage suits in [their] wake." Lawsuits were filed by owners of runaway teams and horses that reached over $85,000. Green eventually settled for under $5,000.

Automobile racing brought the inventor out in Green again. In 1901, he devised a combination telegraph and telephone system composed of a single wire with a water-filled tube placed at the finish line. When a racer crossed the tube, pressure from the automobile's weight caused a spark that instantly stopped the clock. The telegraph recorded the time, and an operator hurriedly telephoned the name of the winning car to the judges. It became the standard method to record finishing times in car racing during the early 1900s.

Less than four years after he drove the first automobile through Texas, Green had accumulated a stable of fine automobiles. One, a large red touring car from France, was given to his mother in New York, complete with chauffeur. It took some time for New Yorkers to absorb the site of Hetty, adorned in her usual black garb, being driven from New Jersey through New York City streets in a shiny, red "Panhard barouche." The frugal Hetty, however, soon returned to travel by train and cabs – if she wasn't walking.

By 1904, Green owned several 12-hp Franklin touring cars and a yellow 21-hp Pope Toledo that became his first racing vehicle. That year he entered the Pope Toledo in a five-mile race sponsored by the fledgling Houston Driving Club. The three entrants were big names of the day – Percy Pierce with his Pierce-Arrow, who took third, another famous inventor – Howard R. Hughes Sr. – who came in second place in a red Peerless, and Green, whose racer took first.

Green was hooked. He continued buying new and faster cars. One was another Pope Toledo called the *Yellow Wasp* that set the 100-mile course speed record in 1905, the other a Packard dubbed *Gray Wolf* that held the fastest one-mile time at under 47 seconds. Preparing for the 1905 summer racing season, he was having three more machines built, including two 100-hp Franklins from Syracuse.

With typical Green exuberance, he began sponsoring races. In the spring of 1905, he spared no expense in bringing his racing fleet to Galveston, attracting some of the top racing talents to test drive his new "champion machines." The raceway, on the Oleander City beach, had some challenges – logs and seaweed had to be cleared, and high tides cut short many races. Mostly, though, the racers complained of horses that bolted into the street whenever the cars sped through town.

1905 was a busy racing year for Green, who entered races in Chicago and New York, planned to open a track between Corpus Christi and Brownsville, and completed another new track at Fair Park in Dallas where he sponsored the world's first 100-mile auto race.

Green was behind a third automobile speed track, called the Gulf of Mexico course, that opened in Galveston in the summer of 1907. That fall, 30 miles of beachfront were manicured for a new straightaway, and for days Green's drivers could be seen trying out his fleet of cars. Speeds of up to 50-mph were anticipated by the contestants. In typical Green fashion, he informed the press of plans to build a grandstand, large café, clubhouse, a five-car garage, and cottages for support staff.

Still pushing the boundaries of automobile racing, in 1909 he promoted an 800-mile race that ended in Dallas in 20-degree temperatures, the drivers braving sleet and snow. Then came the grandest show of them all, the four-day "Big Fair and Auto Carnival" at the San Antonio Fair Grounds, touted as "the greatest race in the history of the Southwest."

It was ironic that the man with so much passion for the automobile could never, for most of his life, drive one. Automobiles had three-foot pedals – one for the gas, another for the brake, and a third for clutch. E.H.R. Green had only one good leg.

Farmer Green. Nothing would eradicate it. Not fire, arsenic-based carcinogens, or the predatory "winged bug" discovered on J.T. Davis's Falls County cotton farm. In the few short years after the boll weevil crossed the border between Mexico and Texas, cotton crops throughout the state were devastated. As yields plummeted, the economic impact affected not only farmers, but shipping, manufacturing, and dozens of other industries that depended on the crop. Particularly hard hit was the profitability of Texas's railroads, and Green's TMR was no exception.

In 1903 Congress took emergency measures, appropriating $250,000 towards eradication of the boll weevil under the auspices of the USDA. That year E.H.R. Green added farmer to his resume. Green invited leading researchers from the USDA and universities to Terrell, offering to pay their expenses and provide them with a research facility. Within weeks, Green acquired 100 acres for an experimental farm south of Terrell that he equipped with a team of mules to work the fields, a large hothouse, and he hired botanist Springer Goes to lead the farm's boll weevil research program.

Between Green's facility and a second experimental farm donated by Walter C. Porter, Terrell became the heart of the boll weevil battle in Texas. It was here that former Iowa State College Professor Seaman A. Knapp proved that a profitable yield could be grown in infected areas. The key, he reported, was an early planting and an early harvest, cutting the stalk before it dried, then burning the field before tilling and replanting.

Green personally conducted some of the basic research, experimenting with different cotton varieties and fertilizers to support Knapp's ideas. The next year, Springer Goes successfully harvested a marginally profitable half a bale to the acre on 65 of Green's acres. Agriculturist Green was elected vice-president of the Texas Farmer's Cooperative Congress.

Green the Florist. Farmer Green watched as the USDA experts, one by one, departed Terrell. His land and the hothouse now empty, he saw an opportunity. Green decided he would convert his experimental cotton farm into a flower farm – not just any flower farm, but the largest horticulture project in the south. Green pumped nearly $300,000 into the new Green Floral Company. He installed a telephone line from the farm to the TMR office, built 20 greenhouses, and dug a well for a reservoir for a novel irrigation design. A pump would move water from the well to the reservoir, then steam pumps would carry water to the greenhouses. Once Green proved the concept, he brought in his TMR chief engineer L.W. Wells to complete the work.

As Wells toiled, his boss had, characteristically, thrown himself into everything flowers. He studied, researched, sought experts, and collected. Following the trail of a rumored new rose variety to Indiana, he had 40,000 shipped to Terrell. Green continued to crisscross the country in search of the most colorful, hardy, or rare, flowering plants. The operation grew to 400 employees who cultivated orchids, roses, carnations, and lilies in greenhouses that eventually covered almost 27 acres. By 1910, his operation netted a profit of $10,000.

The American Pastime. Politics, inventions, finely tuned speedsters, and horticulture were not the only things that kept Green from the Tarpon Club. There was baseball. The young, lame boy, who could only watch as others played ball in Bellows Falls, was now the founder of the Paris baseball team, and in 1906 bought stock in both the Dallas and Houston franchises of the All-Texas League. In 1907, he created the North Texas League – sometimes referred to as the Eddie Green League – a four-club circuit composed of Corsicana, Greenville, Terrell, and Paris. Each of the team towns was located along the tracks of the TMR.

Almost Airborne. Inspired by the feats of Wilbur Wright, who set speed and distance records with his "Model No. 9 aeroplane" in 1908, E.H.R. Green decided he would take to the air. Green ordered his "real, genuine aeroplane" directly from

Wright Brothers in Dayton Ohio, announcing plans to "make a cruise into the upper air of Dallas and Texas at large." Adding 'Pilot Green' to his resume would have been his final diversion before 1910, but it never came to pass. He was summoned that year to New York.

CHAPTER 13

EPILOGUE

At 6-foot-4 and weighing in at 250 pounds, E.H.R. Green could hardly be missed in the halls of New York's Waldorf Astoria that summer day in 1899. He was the only son of Mrs. Hetty Green, who had announced age and hard work was forcing her to take a rest. During her respite, the $80 million Hetty Green empire would be run by her son. It was the first of many times that Hetty, anxious to end Ned's Texas reign and return to New York, would call for him. Green managed to elude his persistent mother's overtures until 1910. That year, he put Texas behind him in his private car as he headed north for New York.

Green was 42 when he set up residence at the Waldorf Astoria Hotel in July 1910. His first order of financial business was the formation of the Westminster Company, a trust designed to lasso in all the pieces of Hetty's financial empire. Although Green was the company's managing director, his mother remained active in the decision-making.

The resume of Edward Howland Robinson Green during the 25 years he would spend mostly in New York, Massachusetts, and Florida was remarkably like that of Texas – a mix of intellectual hobbies with exciting ones, a fascination with technology, a business acumen reminiscent of his mother, and a fondness for young women.

The honorary title of colonel, bestowed upon him in Texas by Governor Colquitt, was now inseparably attached to E.H.R. Green. The boy who started out as Ned, then became the man known to his friends as Eddie, but by everyone else as either

Edward or E.H.R., treasured the title. Associates during his post-Texas years never knew him as anything other Colonel Green, or just 'the Colonel.'

Collector Green. Green was always enamored with collectibles – rare books, jewelry, coins, paper currency, stamps, and erotic pictures. By the mid-1910s, he began collecting in earnest. Of his collecting pursuits, his coin and stamp treasures are the most well-known. Green became one of the world's most renowned coin enthusiasts, or in the words of philatelist Jim Stever, a "massive accumulator." Coin collector Green is best known as the owner of the only 1913 Liberty Head nickels known in existence, seven of the rare 1838-O half dollars, and dozens of high-grade 1796 quarters.

Green's prodigious stamp collection compared to only that of British monarch King George V. His acquisition of the entire sheet of the widely sought, 'Upside Down Jenny's' made him an instant celebrity in and out of stamp circles. In the spring of 1918, as the first 24-cent US postal service airmail prints rolled off the press, no one detected that the subject of the stamp – a Curtiss JN-4 bi-plane – was printed upside down. Washington D.C. stockbroker W.T. Robey noticed – and bought the only sheet before they were pulled from distribution. His $100 investment was worth $15,000 overnight.

Once Green procured the Inverted Jenny's, he sold a few but kept the bulk of them. Mabel once mistook them as regular postage stamps and affixed one of the rarities to an envelope for a letter she posted to her husband. The approximately $4,000 error might have killed his mother, but the affable Green thought it so humorous he had it made into a locket.

After Green's death, it took seven armored trucks to haul his valuables for safekeeping. His stamp collection in the late 1930s was appraised at $1,298,448 and the coins at $1,240,299.

An Honest Woman. One of Hetty's weightiest worries, on a list of anxieties not short, was ensuring that the Green wealth remain within the immediate family. Daughter Sylvia waited until she was 38 before marrying 63-year-old Mathew Astor Wilks in 1909. Lawyers on both sides of their inherited fortunes were only too happy to abide by Hetty's demands for a pre-nuptial contract, one that even carried a signing bonus for the future bridegroom. E.H.R. never broached the subject of marriage while Hetty was living. A year after the wealthiest woman in the world died on July 3, 1916, 48-year-old Colonel E.H.R. Green wed Mabel E. Harlow, 47.

Green was uncharacteristically quiet about his marriage intentions, but in the months before the nuptials, he was busy preparing a wedding present – the largest yacht in the world. It was a gift that almost didn't happen. America was enmeshed in the Great War and ocean-going vessels were in short supply. He settled by rebuilding the Great Lakes steamer *SS United States*, but at 195-feet at the waterline, it was still shorter than J.P. Morgan's yacht *Corsair*. Green solved the problem by welding an additional 60 feet to its steel hull.

After a million-dollar refurbishment at a Brooklyn shipyard, Green's renovated *SS United States* was said to be the costliest privately owned yacht in the world. At 255-feet long and 40-feet wide at the waterline, the ship was powered by 2,500-hp engines lodged in a massive mechanical room. Two smokestacks burned two tons of coal a day just to provide the steam to pressure its plumbing. A technologically advanced navigation system was designed for its pilothouse. Admirers wrote that, with captain, sailors, crew, and staff, it took 71 people to man the ship. The number was closer to 36, but the Colonel was not about to change the perception.

Below decks, Green installed a wireless operating room, "the best cold storage plant ever installed on a yacht or liner," a library, two dining rooms, a drawing room designed as a Louis Quatorze French replica, a living room with a stone fireplace, a Chinese tearoom with a silk rug copied from the Palace of Pekin, and nine master chambers. Green's stateroom was walnut, "distinctly mannish," with telephones connected to every room on a stand beside his bed. Mabel's stateroom was "dainty and queenly," a period reproduction from Maria Antoinette's chambers.

In a nod to his sporting days, Green commissioned a mahogany gun locker filled with gold and nickel-plated custom Colt pistols and Winchester rifles and with the *United States* engraved on the side. Above deck, he mounted four mahogany launches, between 30 and 40-feet long, that he and guests used for fishing, hunting, and pleasure cruising. One, the *Alaska*, was powered by a 130-hp "Speedway engine." According to Doug Wicklund, Green and his visitors entertained themselves by shooting waterfowl from the yacht deck, the crew dropping one of the launches to retrieve any kill.

The July 1917 E.H.R. and Mabel Harlow Green wedding nuptials were celebrated in Illinois. Green never hinted at its coming, and the press raced to cover the story. As had happened many times before, Mr. and Mrs. Green spun an elaborate tale of Mabel's past. The story prepared for the media was that they met through her uncle, George Campbell, when Green was in Chicago on business. Reporters added that, although the bride "did not shine socially," she was devoted to Chicago and New York charities, notably the "Bide a Wee Home," and the Humane Society.

After the small wedding ceremony, new husband Green spoke freely with the press as they crowded the newlywed's private car. He was effusive, but not necessarily honest. "I am marrying a quiet little lady to whom I can go to when I am burdened by the troubles of the world," and to establish "a real home." Then he let them know that the honeymoon would be spent on a cruise aboard the *SS United States*.

That November, former Tarpon Club patriarch E.H.R. Green returned to Aransas Pass. If he shared any recollections as the *SS United States* sailed by the shores of St. Joseph Island, his words went unrecorded. Docked in the Aransas Pass harbor, newspapermen and distinguished visitors prowled the ship's decks, marveling at its opulence. Under the headline "Green's Honeymoon Yacht Now in Harbor," Texas heralded the return of Eddie and Mabel Green. Green told the gathered newsmen that he planned to hunt and fish. It's not known if he ever did – all eyes were fixed on the spectacle of the lavish vessel. Three

142

years later, the great ship sank at Buzzards Bay, near the ancestral Howland-Robinson Round Hill farm in Massachusetts.

For the Colonel, 1917 was an eventful year. He had rebuilt a ship, married, and was still litigating his mother's estate. Since she had left nothing to charity, he and sister Sylvia would split all but about $50,000 of Hetty's $100 million fortune, although there remained the sticky issue of New Jersey and New York's wrangling for a piece of slippery Hetty's inheritance tax. That fall, the Colonel began refurbishing the family estate at Round Hill, Massachusetts.

Round Hill. Located on a peninsula below South Dartmouth on the shores of Buzzards Bay, the Round Hill property had been in the Howland-Robinson family for 200 years. The last occupant of the original Quaker farmhouse with its rambling subsequent additions was Hetty's aunt Sylvia. Hetty rarely visited the property except "to prosecute lawsuits," and after Sylvia's death, the ancestral castle was left to decay.

The *SS United States* passed Long Island Sound as it sailed from New York. Cape Cod Bay lay ahead and the Elizabeth Islands at starboard as the captain made for the jagged granite outcrops and tide-driven coves of the Massachusetts coast. He crossed Buzzards Bay, dropping anchor in the natural harbor of Apponagansett Bay at the edge of Round Hill. The Colonel and his bride had visited the farm in the summer on their honeymoon cruise and decided it was the ideal location to build a great estate. It was now fall of 1918, and he was returning to organize the mammoth undertaking.

Local papers carried advertisements posting jobs for hundreds of builders and laborers. First on the list were stonemasons and carpenters to build the main house. Next were farmers and gardeners to plant peach and apple orchards and crops of corn and potatoes, then other workers needed to clear brush and prepare an expansive, manicured lawn. Using his Texas horticulture expertise, Green crafted two greenhouses and designed an irrigation system for vegetables and flowers.

E.H.R. and Mabel planned to live on the *SS United States* while construction of the residence was underway. A harbor was built for the ship in front of the main house complete with a breakwater and 800-ft pier. It was not occupied for long. In 1920, Green's floating residence struck a rock ledge in Apponagansett Bay and "toppled over."

The grand 60-room stone and marble mansion was completed in 1921 at a cost of $1,500,000. Of its marvels, the one that most captivated Green's attention was his state-of-the-art broadcasting studio. Green had never lost his fascination with wireless telegraphy, and as radio broadcasting evolved in the early 1920s, he was at the forefront. In 1922, he founded the Round Hills Radio Corporation, his company chartered for scientific experimentation in radio, wireless, "new devices," and "the broadcast of music and speech that may be heard with undistorted clearness by far-off listeners."

Company president Green financed the erection of radio towers and, as he had done since his TMR days in Texas, constructed and equipped laboratories. The Massachusetts Institute of Technology Department of Electrical Engineering and other leading science experts of the day were invited to use the facility.

During the summer of 1923, network broadcasters achieved an important milestone by linking independent stations operating at different locations, although the duration of the continuous signal was too short for commercial application. Green, with a team of engineers from AT&T and Western Electric, solved it. That year, he arranged for AT&T to install a telephone line connection from the Round Hills Radio Corporation broadcasting station that enabled WMAF to rebroadcast programs originating from New York City. After a three-month continuous run, Green's WMAF was credited as the first permanent radio network link.

Colonel E.H.R. Green was often the master of ceremonies in nightly radio programs that he opened with the greeting 'The Voice from Way Down East.' The entertainment was not just confined to the airwaves – Green invited the public to his

144

seaside property to listen to music, political speeches, plays, comedy, weather reports and baseball games. As antennas and speaker systems grew both in size and voltage, his programs were blasted across the airwaves for over half a mile. Although his South Dartmouth neighbors no longer had to leave their homes for radio entertainment, not all were pleased.

Then he brought his programs to them. Radio emcee Green took his show on the road from the back of a truck designed with a mobile broadcasting center and a Western Electric public address system, its side panels carrying his WMAF call letters and advertising "The voice from way down east, from the land of the pilgrim fathers." WMAF broadcasts continued each summer until 1928.

Green was not an average radio hobbyist. He understood and contributed not just to broadcast programming, but to such esoteric topics as tropospheric scatter for long-distance communication and high-frequency radio transmissions in aviation guidance systems. Antennas that bristled from the Round Hill grounds in the 1920s were designed to investigate signal strength and radiation patterns. Round Hill's broadcast station even included an experimental radio telescope, built on a water tower designed to look like the foundation of a lighthouse.

The Round Hill harbor originally built for the scrapped *SS United States* gained a new occupant when, in 1924, Green purchased the last remaining 19th-century American whaling vessel, the bark *Charles W. Morgan*. Green was the grandson of one of the ship's earlier owners, Edward Mott Robinson, and the grand sailing craft was the latest in a growing list of Round Hill objects to occupy Green's insatiable curiosity. It took nine months to restore the nautical treasure, after which Green added a whaling village reproduction and blacksmith shop. After Green died, the vessel became part of the Mystic Seaport Museum in Connecticut.

Shorebirds, black ducks, and a smattering of mallards scattered from the salt marsh pond on the property every time Herbert Hill's small plane took off or landed, and the ruts he made on the manicured lawn drove the gardeners to distraction. The Colonel wasn't bothered by any of it. He relished the sound and spectacle of aviation and immediately decided to build an airport.

In usual Green fashion, no costs were spared as buildings were razed or relocated and a hangar constructed. More than 170,000 cubic yards of topsoil and sand pumped from Buzzards Bay were moved into the marsh, the wetlands filled and leveled for two runways. A year later, in 1928, the private Round Hill airfield was ready. The man who made the first tire ruts, Herbert "Bert" Hill, was hired as airport manager and ran a flight school on the grounds.

With improvements such as runway approach lights and a rotating beacon with enormous letters spelling 'Round Hill' on the Green mansion roof, Green's airport was the pride of New England fliers. A polished Pierce Arrow truck delivered free gasoline to airfield visitors such as Eddie Rickenbacker with his single wing Fokker Super Universal, William Randolph Hearst Jr.'s Sikorsky S39, and other famed fliers who touched down on its manicured grass runways. As renowned aviator Charles Lindbergh tracked one false lead after another following his son's kidnapping, he landed at Round Hill to investigate a rumor that the child was being held at nearby Martha's Vineyard. The tip proved to be a hoax.

Colonel Green's fascination with flight included purchase of "a flying boat", the *Miami Maid*, and he built a seaplane ramp and a special tracked hanger for it. There was the 130-foot-long Goodyear blimp *Mayflower*, used not just for pleasure but by the Massachusetts Institute of Technology in its experimental radar research and meteorological studies, that was berthed in the airport's giant hangar. When the hangar space was vacated, it housed MIT's 40-foot high 'Van de Graaff generator.' De Graff's innocuously titled electrical experiments were actually studies in the field of subatomic particle acceleration to bombard atomic nuclei. Green was fascinated by it.

Florida. The Colonel and Mabel spent their winters in Florida after they bought the former Star Island Yacht Club on 3.5 acres overlooking Miami's Biscayne Bay in 1924. A fleet of new seafaring purchases graced the bulkhead. The latest *Mabel*, a speed cruiser, was joined by the 120-foot and 130-foot luxury yachts *Pioneer* and, in a nod to his honorary title, the *Colonel*. The most unusual vessel was the *Isola Stella*, its 52-foot hull designed as a mix of "gondola and Spanish Galleon" that, below decks, featured a music room and typical for Green, a broadcasting station. The eccentric vessel was used primarily to ferry guests from Star Island to the exclusive Miami Beach Bath Club.

The main residence was remodeled in a Spanish mission-style, with red tile roof and second-floor balconies, and surrounded by a profusion of tropical flowers and stately royal palms. Author Arthur H. Lewis wrote that the east wing of the Star Island estate featured a room used for viewing moving pictures, the reels of its projector fed from a nearby vault that held Green's vast collection of pornographic films, which, like his collections of stamps and coins, was among the best in the world.

The dozen small rooms off the main hallway – special rooms as they were called – were occupied by "Uncle Ned" and Mabel's protégés, the young women on the payroll labeled – to those not in the Green's inner circle – as secretaries or typists. Biographers are convinced that, in the early years of their marriage, their relationship with these women was, in part, sexual. In later years, their association was probably mostly platonic. Mabel seemed to understand E.H.R.'s need to be surrounded by young women, the paternal Ned taking a particular interest in selecting the girl's fashions, makeup, and hairstyles, and offering to pay for their college. It was quite a spectacle as E.H.R. and Mabel traveled between Miami and Round Hill, the trip requiring two passenger cars and one baggage car to handle the Green entourage.

Return to Bellow Falls. Colonel Edward Howland Robinson Green died on June 8, 1936, at Lake Placid, New York. Fifteen hundred well-wishers gathered to pay their respects along the tracks as his remains were taken from Round Hill to the family

147

plot in Bellows Falls, Vermont, where his father had buried the teenage boy's amputated leg. A half-century later, Green and his leg were reunited.

Colonel Green may have been gone, but the legacy of his fortune would persist. Initially estimated at $80 million the actual figure was between $36 and $44 million. First in line for a share of the tax pie was the federal government, which took a $17,521,000 cut. Next on the list were the states of New York, Massachusetts, Texas, and Florida. Each of the defendant states claimed Green as a resident, the ensuing litigation so tangled that it was decided by US Supreme Court, which hired Special Master John S. Flannery to hold hearings in each state to determine Green's domicile.

E.H.R. Green largely abandoned Texas after he moved north in 1910. Between 1911 and 1927, he made no more than one or two trips to Texas each year. But he voted in Texas and told people that "I have never changed my legal residence from Terrell, Texas." Although his visits stopped altogether after he sold the Texas Midland Railroad in 1928, Texas had high hopes when it was her turn in Flannery's proceedings.

Special Master Flannery held the Lone Star State hearing at the Dallas Adolphus Hotel. In Tom Peeler's colorful account, "the Texas attorney general paraded all of Ned's old cronies through the witness box to prove that Ned died a Texan. Gooseneck Bill and the other old-timers told how Ned always used to say that he was born a Quaker and educated a Catholic and did business as a Jew, but that he would always be a Texan." The court also heard that "a cork leg had been discovered in a Terrell apartment," and it was entered as evidence.

The Special Master did not rule in Texas's favor. Flannery, in his decision, wrote that Green had not abided in, or had active connections with, the Lone Star State for some time. He went on to say that Green's motive for a multiplicity of residences was solely to avoid taxation, and ruled Green was a resident of Massachusetts at the time of his death.

A concurrent estate battle was fought between his widow Mabel Harlow and his sister Sylvia Ann Wilks. Green had persuaded Mabel to sign a prenuptial agreement for a one-time $625,000 payment and a lifetime stipend of $1,500 a month. Now, claiming that she didn't know what she was signing, Mabel wanted a bigger piece. For her part, Sylvia produced a will signed by her brother in 1908. In it, he left everything to his sister. Contested in New York, the rival claimants eventually settled with Mabel receiving another $500,000.

The passing of Mrs. Mabel Harlow Green in April 1950 made few headlines. Sylvia Green Wilks died the following February. In her last years, Sylvia began to acquire the idiosyncrasies of her famous mother. She dressed in black and lived in isolation, both in a Fifth Avenue apartment "jammed with old Green furniture," or her vast, disheveled Greenwich Connecticut estate 'Alta Crest.'

Sylvia's residences also had eerie similarities to those of her mother. She saved money by disconnecting her telephones. Situated next to her late brother's prominently displayed wheelchair was a wood-burning stove she preferred to paying for expensive fuel oil. The paper flowers arranged in vases throughout the residence, less costly than real blossoms, were another cost-saving move she learned from her mother.

It seems ironic that, after all the years of financial combat, both of Hetty Green's children died without children of their own. The Green fortune, now estimated at $100 million, was distributed per the terms of Sylvia's will. The money went to dozens of charities.

The Last Leg. The car nosed into the main drive at Round Hill, the youngster eyeing the familiar cornfields between Smith Neck Road and the Round Hill barn before reaching the semi-circular driveway bounded on each side by manicured privet hedges. He was hired as summer help, and those hedges were his responsibility. It took him nearly a month to cut them all. If it was foggy, which it almost always was, he occupied himself instead with indoor tasks. It was the 1960s, and future Cape Cod school teacher Bob Geary remembers Round Hill vividly from

149

his summer job, some 30 years after the passing of Colonel E.H.R. Green.

The Van de Graaff generator was gone, moved to the Boston Museum of Science. So was the *Charles W. Morgan*, now berthed at the Mystic Seaport Museum in Connecticut along with parts of the Colonel's whaling village exhibit. The long-abandoned Howland farmhouse was still visible, decrepit from neglect. Next to the Colonel's six-car garage, empty except for a 1935 Packard Woodie station wagon, was a small pond that Bob remembers held the largest snapping turtle he'd ever seen in his life.

Some of the Colonel's radio antennas still rose from the roof of the main house and surrounding hills. The WMAF broadcast building that sourced "the voice from way down east" had been long silenced, and was now headquarters for MIT's defense contract research, known simply as "the Diffusion Project" by locals. The enormous concrete swimming pool by the beach remained, its empty cement orifice the place where MIT's Tech Christian Association set up their barbeque pits during the summer.

A few people living at Round Hill persisted since the Green's days, including aviator Bert Hill and his wife Priscilla. Hill was now the estate caretaker along with Dick Van Stone. One building on the grounds was divided into apartments for the MIT staff, including Bob's brother Harry and his family who occupied the apartment where the Colonel's chauffer once lived. Other diffusion project research scientists came and went before they all disappeared in the summer of 1965, relocated north of Boston.

Passing through the massive balcony and entrance hall of the Round Hill mansion, the first floor was mostly vacant except for the ballroom and living room, lined with surplus floor-to-ceiling computers abandoned by MIT's Lincoln Laboratory. The third floor still had its dormitory-style rooms once used by the Colonel's staff and his 'wards,' but all vestiges of the life they lived were expunged. In the basement behind the elevator was a storage room filled with boxes of letters the Colonel

150

received requesting money. "There must have been a thousand," Bob remembers, "some never opened."

On the second floor were more bedrooms. Here, the 'Chinese room' looked as it did when the Green's left. Other rooms were stacked with cartons of junk and boxes of photographs and slides left by the Colonel. Bill Sheehan had charge of the piles of obsolete Lincoln Lab equipment occupying part of the second floor. He was so fanatical to the details of his inventory that, when two Collins receivers went missing, he drove home to Padanaram and closed the garage door. He died there with his car running.

MIT eventually exchanged the Round Hill estate for some prime real estate in Cambridge. The Catholic Archdiocese, Bob remembers, then "turned the big house into a rabbit warren of something like 200 cells." Today it is home to multimillion dollar condominiums. The Green beachfront now belongs to the town, which they managed to wrangle into their possession through eminent domain.

One of Bob's recollections is of the adoptive parents of a childhood friend who received a gift of $100,000, and they never knew why. It turned out to be a gift from Sylvia Astor Green Wilks. He also recalls how the staff gathered around as new employees went through their Round Hill initiation. They were instructed to fetch a large box from a high shelf in the basement, Bob says, and open it. It was a rite of passage, and it contained the Colonel's only remaining prosthetic leg.

Collector Green's prodigious stamp collection compared to only that of British monarch King George V. One of his most publicized collections was that of the Inverted Jenny, the 24-cent United States postage stamp first issued on May 10, 1918, in which the image of the Curtiss JN-4 airplane in the center of the design was erroneously printed upside-down. Stamp collector William T. Robey purchased the only sheet with the error at the post office. Robey sold the sheet to noted Philadelphia dealer Eugene Klein for $15,000. Klein announced that the entire sheet had been purchased by an individual collector. That buyer, who paid $20,000, was Colonel E.H.R. Green donated one 'Jennie' to the Red Cross in support of its war efforts (which was auctioned off for $300), while retaining forty-one of the stamps in his own collection, including the plate-number block (initially eight stamps) and several blocks of four. The remainder of the inverts were sold off at steadily increasing prices through Klein, who kept a block of four for himself. https://thexodirectory.blogspot.com/2007/12/rare-jenny-stamp-with-upside-down.html.

152

More grimaces than smiles on the wedding day of Sylvia Green to Mathew
Astor Wilks in 1909. Hetty Green is to left. Library of Congress, Prints &
Photographs Division, No. LC-USZ62-86682, https://lccn.loc.gov/
2002715419.

E.H.R. and Mabel, pictured in the early 1920s, were married in 1916. After Green left Texas, he nearly always used the honorary title of "Colonel," bestowed on him by Texas governor Colquitt. Collection of Jim Moloney.

Colonel Green presented his wife Mabel with world's largest private yacht, the *SS United States*, as a wedding present. Shown is one of Green's gold and nickel-plated Winchester Model 1890 rifles from the ill-fated yacht. From: A Sea-Going Arsenal: Guns of the Yacht United States, Doug Wicklund, June 12, 2017, https://www.nrablog.com/articles/ 2017/6/a-sea-going-arsenal-guns-of-the-yacht-united-states/.

Colonel Green's yacht *SS United States,* was the costliest and longest
privately owned yacht in the world. At 255-feet long, and 40-feet wide at the
waterline, the ship was powered by two 2,500-hp engines. While the Green's
were building their grand manor house at the ancestral Howland-Robinson
Round Hill farm in Massachusetts in 1920, the *SS United States* struck a rock
and "toppled over" at Apponagansett Bay. Photos courtesy New Bedford
Whaling Museum.

Photo postcard Colonel E.H.R. Green's 60-room Round Hill manor house, in South Dartmouth, Massachusetts. Collection of Jim Moloney.

Radio emcee E.H.R. Green and "The Voice from Way Down East" broadcasting from his Round Hill studio, WMAF. Green's WMAF was credited as the first permanent radio network link, and the Colonel was often the master of ceremonies in nightly radio programs. Collection of Jim Moloney.

E.H.R. Green in his electric car on the Round Hill grounds, with the mansion as a backdrop. In the distance are radio towers and, to the right, his public address system. Courtesy of Boston Public Library, Leslie Jones Collection, No. 08-06-009331, https://ark.digitalcommonwealth.org/ark:/ 50959/ 5x21 tp026.

The *Charles W. Morgan* whaling ship, named for owner Charles Waln Morgan. Launched in 1841, the ship made 37 voyages over some 80 years. E.H.R. Green was approached to restore the ship not only for its historical importance, but because it was a family heirloom, once co-owned by Green's grandfather's company. Green had the ship towed to his Round Hill estate and, with New Bedford philanthropist John Duff, founded 'Whaling Enshrined' to raise funds for its restoration and exhibition at Green's estate. Green held a dedication ceremony on the 86th anniversary of the ship's launch and gave her to 'Whaling Enshrined' on July 21, 1926. After Green died, the vessel became part of the Mystic Seaport Museum in Connecticut. Collection of Jim Moloney.

Aerial view looking the northwest from the pier with the restored whaling ship *Charles M. Morgan* across part of the Round Hill landing field. Herbert 'Bert' Hill's aviation school building is to left of the ship's bow, the greenhouses in the distance, and the Goodyear blimp hangar is to right. The Colonel shared his estate with scientists and aviators, and invited the public to visit the *Charles M. Morgan* and use the beach and Round Hill facilities. Courtesy of Boston Public Library, Leslie Jones Collection, No. 08-06-005718, https://ark.digitalcommon wealth.org/ark:/50959/cn69mj00z.

E.H.R. and Mabel Green in Green's experimental electrical car at Round Hill airfield, which was opened in 1928. The two men on left and right are unidentified. Courtesy of University of Massachusetts Amherst Libraries, Special Collections and University Archives, Alton H. Blackington Collection, No. 061/muph061-sl321-i002.

E.H.R. Green was at home behind the wheel of machines on land, sea, and in the air. This image is of 'Aviator Green,' at Round Hill airfield, Massachusetts. Courtesy of University of Massachusetts Amherst Libraries, Special Collections and University Archives, Alton H. Blackington Collection, No. PH 061/muph061-sl320-i001.

In 1929 General Electric developed an electronic transmission device, which eliminated the need for a clutch when driving an automobile. One such auto was delivered to Colonel Green for testing at Round Hill. For the first time Green was able to drive a gasoline-powered car. In a 1929 article, the writer observed that Colonel Green was so pleased with the vehicle "that he has ordered a second with a limousine body, and is planning a third, of the touring-car type." Collection of Jim Moloney.

Photo postcard of Colonel E.H.R. Green's Star Island, Miami Beach estate. The main residence was remodeled in a Spanish mission-style, with red tile roof and second-floor balconies, and surrounded by a profusion of tropical flowers and stately royal palms. Curiously, there are no postcards featuring Green's Tarpon Club at Sport, Texas. Collection of Jim Moloney.

Mrs. Mabel Harlow Green in 1936, soon after the death of her husband Ned. The passing of Mabel in 1950 made few newspaper headlines. Collection of Jim Moloney.

REFERENCES

BEGINNINGS
Percy B. St. John, "Wild Sports in the Far West," *New Sporting Magazine,* 10 no. 50 (1845): 384-7.
Galveston Daily News, Dec. 3, 1876.
Galveston Daily News, May 15, 1879.
San Antonio Light, Nov. 12, 1885.
Murphy Givens, "Village on St. Joseph's was a Victim of War," *Caller-Times*, Dec. 6, 2006, http://www.caller.com/news/2006/dec/06/village-on-st-josephs-was-a-victim-of-the-war/.
Keith Guthrie, *History of Aransas Pass,* Unpublished, Collection of R.K. Sawyer.
Tom W. Stewart, "History of the Aransas Pass Jetties," Unpublished, Collection of Jim Moloney.
Craig H. Roell, *"Lea, Pryor,"* Handbook of Texas Online, https://www.tshaonline.org/handbook/entries/lea-pryor.
19th Century Steamships, Bureau of Safety and Environmental Enforcement, https://www.bsee.gov/site-page/19th-century-steamships.
John Guthrie Ford, "Island's Rich in Maritime History," https://portaransasmuseum.org/island_history/islands-rich-in-maritime-history/.
"Taming the Channel III: The Pass Must Be Caught," Port Aransas Preservation and Historical Association., https://portaransasmuseum.org/exhibits/taming-the-channel-the-pass-must-be-caught/.
Charles E. Pearson and Joe J. Simmons, "Underwater Archaeology of the Wreck of the Steamship *Mary* (41NU252) and Assessment of Seven Anomalies, Corpus Christi Entrance Channel, Nueces County Texas."

BECOMING E.H.R. GREEN
Quincy Daily Journal, May 27, 1887.
Saint Paul Daily Globe, May 27, 1887.
St. Paul Globe, Sept. 11, 1898.
The Howland Will Case, The American Law Register (1852-1891) 38, no. 9 (1890): 562–81, https://doi.org/10.2307/3305329.
Carroll Herald, Jan. 3. 1906.
San Antonio Light, July 23,1916.
Amarillo Sunday News, April 27, 1930.
Port Arthur News, Nov. 15, 1936.

Peter Wyckoff, "Queen Midas: Hetty Robinson Green," *The New England Quarterly* 23, no. 2 (1950): 147–71, https://doi.org/10.2307/362074.

Lewis, Arthur H., *The Day They Shook the Plum Tree* (New York: Harcourt Brace, 1963).

Commerce Journal, Oct. 9, 1975.

Slack, Charles, *Hetty, the Genius and Madness of America's First Female Tycoon* (New York: Harper Collins, 2004).

Wallach, Janet, *The Richest Woman in America* (New York: Doubleday, 2012).

"The Witch, the Wench & the Colonel," *William Bryk's Chronicles of Old New York*, https://cityofsmoke.wordpress.com/tag/colonel-e-h-r-green/

BEING E.H.R. GREEN

Galveston Daily News, March 8, 1895.

San Antonio Daily Light, May 23, 1895.

Henry Hall, Ed., *America's Successful Men of Affairs* (New York: Tribune Printing Co., 1895).

Sterling Evening Gazette, June 29, 1896.

San Antonio Daily Light, Sept. 17, 1896.

Boston Post, Aug. 19, 1899.

El Paso Daily Herald, March 22, 1901.

Brownsville Daily Herald, March 22, 1901.

Washington Times, Jan. 28, 1902.

New York Times, Jan. 28, 1911.

Lewis, Arthur H., *The Day They Shook the Plum Tree* (New York: Harcourt Brace, 1963).

Commerce Journal, Oct. 9, 1975.

Tom Peeler, "Nostalgia, Ned and Mabel," *D Magazine*, December 1984, https://www.dmagazine.com/publications/d-magazine/1984/december/nostalgia-ned-and-mabel/.

Maxine Holmes and Gerald D. Saxon, Eds., *The WPA Dallas Guide and History* (Dallas Public Library and Univ. North Texas Press, 1992), https://texashistory.unt.edu/ark:/67531/metadc28336/manifest/

Slack, Charles, *Hetty, the Genius and Madness of America's First Female Tycoon* (New York: Harper Collins, 2004).

Wallach, Janet, *The Richest Woman in America* (New York: Doubleday, 2012).

S.G. Reed, "Texas Midland Railroad," *Handbook of Texas Online*, https://www.tshaonline.org./handbook/entries/texas-midland-railroad.

"The Witch, the Wench & the Colonel," *William Bryk's Chronicles of Old New York*, https://cityofsmoke.wordpress.com/tag/colonel-e-h-r-green/

"William Madison McDonald (1866-1950)," *Black Past*, https://www.blackpast.org/african-american-history/mcdonald-william-madison-1866-1950/.

THE AMERICAN SPORTSMAN
Galveston Daily News, Aug. 9, 1885.
San Antonio Daily Light, March 28, 1888.
Jacksboro Gazette, Feb. 9, 1899.
Galveston Daily News, Feb. 10, 1889.
Galveston Daily News, June 1, 1890.
San Antonio Daily Express, June 2, 1890.
San Antonio Daily Express, June 12, 1890.
San Antonio Daily Express, Jan. 4, 1893.
Dallas Morning News, Sept. 25, 1898.
Harris, William C., Ed., *American Angler* (New York: Outing Publishing) 29 no. 1 (1899): 4.
Outing Magazine, Vol. XLI, Oct. 1902-March (1903).
Orange Daily Tribune, June 9, 1904.
San Antonio Daily Light, March 4, 1905.
Edward H. Hudson, "The Giant of the Mexican Gulf," Outing Magazine, Vol. XLV, Oct. 1904-March 1905.
A.W. Dimock, *The Book of the Tarpon* (New York: Outing Publishing Co., 1911).
Holder, Charles Frederic, *Science*, Vol. XLII, No. 1093 (1915): 823-4.
Sawyer, R.K, *Images of the Hunt* (Houston: Kemp Publishing, 2020).
"Antique Fishing Reels," https://antiquefishingreels.com/casting-reels/vom-hofe-julius-3/.
"Antique Fishing Reels," https://antiquefishingreels.com/salt-water-reels/vom-hofe-edward/.
"Antique Fishing Reels," https://antiquefishingreels.com/vintage-rods/vom-hofe-edward-new-york-n-y/.
"Antique Fishing Rods," https://www.collectorsweekly.com/fishing/rods
Ed Pritchard, "History and Evolution: Gig Game Fishing's Golden Years," https://antiquefishingreels.com/big-game-reels/history-evolution/
"Fishing Reel History," *ORCA*, https://www.orcaonline.org/reel-facts/reel-history/.
"The History of the O'Shaughnessy Fish Hook," https://finandflame.com/the-history-of-the-oshaugnessy-fish-hook/.
Tom Green, "Antique Reels," http://www.antiquereels.com/articles/History-of-reel-makers-in-this-collection.htm
"Silver King: The Birth of Big Game Fishing," *WGCU Fishing Documentary*, https://www.youtube.com/watch?v=nKeJQb8jhgA&t=878s.

CREATING THE TARPON CLUB

Sunday Gazetteer, Feb. 11, 1894.
Galveston Daily News, Feb. 11, 1895.
Dallas Morning News, Nov. 24, 1895.
Brownsville Daily Herald, Dec. 22, 1896.
Forest and Stream, Sept. 17 (1898): 230.
Galveston Daily News, May 21, 1897.
Baltimore Sun, June 3, 1898.
Galveston Daily News, June 29, 1898.
El Paso Daily Herald, July 6, 1898.
El Paso Herald, July 19, 1898.
Galveston Daily News, Aug. 15, 1898.
San Antonio Daily Express, Aug. 28, 1898.
Brownsville Daily Herald, Sept. 2, 1898.
San Antonio Light, Sept. 11, 1898.
San Antonio Daily Light, Sept. 11, 1898.
San Antonio Daily Light, Sept. 15, 1898.
Dallas Morning News, Sept. 25, 1898.
Galveston Daily News, Sept. 27, 1898.
Galveston Daily News, Aug. 15, 1898.
Albany News, Nov.11, 1898.
Galveston Tribune, Nov. 14, 1898.
Houston Daily Post, Nov. 16, 1898.
Galveston Daily News, Nov. 18, 1898.
Yoakum Daily Herald, Nov. 18, 1898.
Brownsville Daily Herald, Nov. 22, 1898.
El Paso Daily Herald, Nov. 22, 1898.
Galveston Daily News, Jan. 10, 1899.
Dallas Morning News, Jan. 11, 1899.
San Antonio Sunday Light, Feb.12, 1899.
San Antonio Daily Light, March 8, 1899.
Shiner Gazette, April 12, 1899.
San Antonio Daily Express, June 18,1899.
Dallas Morning News, Dec. 17, 1899.
Forest and Stream, Vol. LV, July-Dec. 1900 (New York: Forest and Stream Publishing Co., 1900): 409.
New York Times, Oct. 19, 1902.

OPERATING THE TARPON CLUB

Piddington, Henry, 1848. The Sailors' Horn Book For the Law of Storms. (New York: John Wiley): 7.
Houston Daily Post, June 2, 1898.
San Antonio Daily Light, June 20, 1898.

Corpus Christi Caller-Times, May 5, 1899.
El Paso Herald, July 19, 1898.
Sunday Gazetteer, Aug. 7, 1898.
Dallas Morning News, Sept. 25, 1898.
San Antonio Daly Light, March 3, 1899.
Galveston Daily News, April 2, 1899.
"1900 United States Federal Census," Schedule No. 1, *National Archives and Records Administration,* District 1, Aransas, Rockport, https://www.ancestry.com/discoveryui-content/view/70110109:7602.
"Annual Report of the United States Life-Saving Service for the Fiscal Year Ending June 20, 1900" (Washington: Govt. Printing Office, 1901): 50.
Price, W. Armstrong, *Hurricanes Affecting the Coast of Texas From Galveston to Rio Grande,* Technical Memorandum No. 78, U.S. Dept. of the Army Corps of Engineers (1956): 3.
Rex H. "Jim" Stever, "Sport Texas PO," *Texas Postal History Society Journal,* 40 no. 3 (2015).
Dennis L. Noble, "A Legacy: The United States Life-Saving Service," http://n.b5z.net/i/u/10059514/f/articles/AHistoryoftheUSLSS-DenisNoble.pdf.
Life-Saving Service & Coast Guard Stations, United States Coast Guard, http://www.uscg.mil/history/stations/StationIndex.asp.
"History of the National Weather Service," *National Weather Service,* http://www.weather.gov/timeline.
Jerry Proc, "Brief History of Naval Radio Communications and Signals Intelligence in the Royal Canadian Navy," http://www.jproc.ca/rrp/nro_his.html.
I.E. Tannehill, "The Hurricane," U.S. Dept. of Ag., Miscellaneous Publication 197, July 1934, (Washington D.C.: US Govt. Printing Office, 1934): 7.
Allen, William and Taylor, Sue Hastings, *Aransas: The Life of a Texas Coastal County,* (Austin: Eakin Press, 1997): 240-62.

BELONGING TO THE TARPON CLUB

Forest and Stream, Vol. XLIII (New York: Forest and Stream Publishing Co., N.Y., 1894): 448.
Baltimore Sun, June 3, 1898.
El Paso Herald, July 19, 1898.
Sunday Gazetteer, Aug. 7, 1898.
Galveston Daily News, Aug. 15, 1898.
Jacksboro Gazette, Feb. 9, 1899.
San Antonio Daily Light, Dec. 17, 1899.
Burnet Bulletin, Sept. 27, 1900.

San Antonio Sunday Light, Dec. 9. 1900.
El Paso Daily Herald, March 22, 1901.
Galveston Daily News, Oct. 19. 1902.
St. Louis Republic, Feb. 1, 1903.
Port Arthur Herald, Nov. 21, 1903.
Baltimore Sun, Jan. 18, 1904.
Dallas Morning News, March 2, 1904
San Antonio Daily Light, Oct. 30. 1904.
Dallas Morning News, Dec. 24, 1905.
New York Times, June 17, 1906.
Brownsville Daily Herald, Nov. 21, 1906.
Brownsville Daily Herald, July 12, 1907.
Galveston Daily News, Nov. 22, 1907.
Brownsville Daily Herald, Nov. 16, 1908.
Mount Vernon Lawrence Chieftain, March 18, 1909.
Los Angeles Herald, July 24, 1909.
Washington Times, July 24, 1909.
Midland Journal, July 30, 1909.
Chicago Saturday Blade, Oct. 30, 1909.
Herbert Whyte, "Herbert Whyte and His Answers," *The Outing Magazine* no. 54 (1909): 509.
Los Angeles Herald, Jan. 5, 1910.
Decatur Wise County Messenger, Feb. 4, 1910.
New York Times, April 17, 1910.
Brownsville Herald, Jan. 28, 1911.
Dallas Morning News, Sept. 7, 1924.
Port Arthur News July 19, 1925.
Dallas Morning News, Feb. 11, 1962.
Dallas Morning News, June 23, 1963.
Shel Arensen, "Great African Baloonograph Safari Fizzles, Old Africa: Stories from East Africa's Past," (2009), https://oldafricamagazine.com/great-african-baloonograph-safari-fizzles/.
Sawyer, R.K, *A Hundred Years of Texas Waterfowl Hunting* (College Station: A&M Univ. Press, 2012).

COASTAL BEND HUNTING
Dallas Morning News, Nov. 15, 1892.
Dallas Morning News, Nov. 25, 1892.
Dallas Morning News, Nov. 24, 1893.
Emerson Hough, "Dixie Land," *Forest and Stream*, April 7, 1894: 292-3.

Emerson Hough, "The Sunny South," *Forest and Stream*, April 20, 1895: 304-5.

"The Sunny South," *Forest and Stream*, May 1895: 367.

Dallas Morning News, Nov. 24, 1895.

Dallas Morning News, Feb. 5, 1897.

Galveston Daily News, Jan. 16, 1898.

Galveston Daily News, Feb. 22, 1898.

Dallas Morning News, June 29, 1898.

San Antonio Daily Express, Nov. 23, 1899.

W.B. Leffingwell, "Shooting on the Gulf Coast," *An Illustrated Monthly Magazine of Sport, Travel and Recreation*, 33 (1899): 506-509.

Galveston Daily News, Feb. 11, 1900.

F.S. Monnett, *American Canoe Association, League of American Sportsmen*, (New York: George O. Shields) 13 no. 6 (1900): 460.

New York Times, Oct. 19, 1902.

"Ducks on the Texas Coast," *Hunter-Trader-Trapper,* 17 no. 3 (1908): 75-6.

Daily Advocate, Jan. 25, 1915.

Galveston Daily News, April 23, 1917.

San Antonio Express, Oct. 29, 1929.

Huson, Hobart, *History of Refugio County* (Houston: Guardsman Publishing Co., 1956), 2:172.

Sawyer, R.K, *A Hundred Years of Texas Waterfowl Hunting* (College Station: A&M Univ. Press, 2012).

Sawyer, R.K, *Texas Market Hunting* (College Station: A&M Univ. Press, 2013).

COASTAL BEND FISHING

San Antonio Daily Express, Sept. 28, 1888.

Galveston Daily News, June 1, 1890.

San Antonio Daily Express, June 2, 1890.

Forest and Stream, Jan. 26, 1895: 68.

Dallas Morning News, Sept. 25, 1898.

San Antonio Light, June 26, 1898.

The American Angler, Vol. XXIX, no. 1, Jan. 1899: 29.

Jno. A. Sea, "Among the Texas Tarpon," *The American Angler*, Vol. XXIX, no. 1, Jan. 1899: 172.

Jacksboro Gazette, Feb. 9, 1899.

San Antonio Daily Express, June 18,1899.

San Antonio Daily Light, Dec. 17, 1899.

Nellie D.S. Graham, "Tarpon Fishing at Aransas Pass," *Outing Magazine*, Vol. VII, 1898-1900: 474.

Traverse City Morning Record, Sept. 11, 1900.
Sterling Evening Gazette, Sept. 11, 1900.
Galveston Daily News, Sept. 13, 1900.
San Antonio Daily Light, Nov. 15, 1900.
Forest and Stream, Vol. LV, 1900, July-Dec. 1900 (New York: Forest and Stream Publishing Co., 1900): 409.
Emerson Hough, "Chicago and the West," *Forest and Stream*, Vol. LVI, April 13, 1901: 290.
Washington Times, Jan. 28, 1902.
San Antonio Light, June 7, 1902.
New York Times, Oct. 19, 1902.
Outing Magazine, Vol. XLI, Oct. 1902-March 1903.
Edward H. Hudson, "The Giant of the Mexican Gulf," *Outing Magazine*, Vol. XLV, Oct. 1904-March 1905.
Charles Frederick Holder, "The High Leapers," *Outing Magazine*, 10, 1905-6: 602-7.
Isaac M. Cline, "Special Report on the Galveston Hurricane, September 8, 1900," *in* David Roth, *NOAA History – Stories and Tales of the Weather Service/Storm Tales/Galveston Storm of 1900*, www.history.noaa.gov.

COASTAL BEND YACHTING

Galveston Daily News, July 4, 1892.
Evening Tribune, Aug. 4, 1892.
Galveston Daily News, Aug. 13, 1892.
Galveston Daily News, Aug. 20, 1892.
Forest and Stream, April 7, 1894: 292-3.
Galveston Daily News, Sept. 2, 1894.
Shiner Gazette, May 26, 1897.
Galveston Daily News, June 30, 1897.
Galveston Daily News, July 9, 1897.
Galveston Daily News, July 10, 1897.
Houston Daily Post, July 13, 1897.
Houston Daily Post, Sept. 25, 1898.
Corpus Christi Caller, May 26, 1899.
Galveston Daily News, Jan. 25, 1902.
San Antonio Daily Light, June 13, 1902.
San Antonio Daily Light, June 15, 1902.
Houston Post, June 17, 1902.
San Antonio Daily Light, Aug. 25, 1903.
Allen, William and Taylor, Sue Hastings, *Aransas: The Life of a Texas Coastal County*, (Austin: Eakin Press, 1997): 432.

ENDING THE TARPON CLUB

San Antonio Sunday Light, June 17, 1900.
Galveston Daily News, Aug. 3, 1900.
Bryan Eagle, Aug. 9, 1900.
San Antonio Sunday Light, Sept. 2, 1900.
Galveston Daily News, Sept. 6, 1900.
San Antonio Daily Light, Sept 11, 1900.
The Democrat, Oct. 11, 1900.
San Antonio Daily Light, Oct. 15, 1900.
Brownsville Daily Herald, Oct. 20, 1900.
Brownsville Daily Herald, March 22, 1901.
St. Louis Republic, Jan. 29, 1902.
San Antonio Sunday Light, Nov. 9, 1902.
Orange Daily Tribune, June 9, 1904.
Houston Post, June 25, 1904.
Corpus Christi-Caller, July 15, 1904.
San Antonio Daily Light, Aug. 20, 1904.
Galveston Daily News, Oct. 25, 1904.
Corpus Christi-Caller, Nov. 25, 1904.
Galveston Daily News, April 28, 1905.
Robert Conley, "Sport Texas – A Luxurious Life, A Disinterested Death," *Journal of Texas Philately & Postal History*, Aug. 2021: 6-10.

LIFE AFTER THE TARPON CLUB

Boston Post, Aug. 19, 1899.
San Antonio Sunday Light, June 17, 1900.
Galveston Daily News, Aug. 3, 1900.
Bryan Eagle, Aug. 9, 1900.
San Antonio Sunday Light, Sept. 2, 1900.
Galveston Daily News, Sept. 6, 1900.
San Antonio Daily Light, Sept 11, 1900.
San Antonio Daily Light, Oct. 15, 1900.
Brownsville Daily Herald, Oct. 20, 1900.
Brownsville Daily Herald, March 22, 1901.
Galveston Tribune, March 11, 1902.
San Antonio Sunday Light, Nov. 9, 1902.
Boston Globe, June 8, 1903.
Houston Post, Nov. 13, 1903.
Schulenberg Sticker, Dec. 3, 1903.
San Antonio Daily Light, Aug. 20, 1904.
Houston Post, Oct. 20, 1904.
Southern Mercury, Oct. 20, 1904.

Galveston Daily News, Oct. 25, 1904.
Houston Post, Nov. 24, 1904.
1904 Texas Almanac (A.H. Belo & Co., 1904).
Corpus Christi Caller, March 17, 1905.
Galveston Daily News, April 28, 1905.
Galveston Daily News, May 1, 1905.
San Antonio Daily Light, May 4, 1905.
Galveston Daily News, July 8, 1905.
Southern Mercury and Farmers Union Password, July 13, 1905.
El Paso Sunday Times, Feb. 18, 1906.
San Antonio Daily Light, Aug. 17, 1906.
Liberty Vindicator, Sept. 14, 1906.
Galveston Daily News, Sept. 23, 1906.
San Antonio Daily Light, Oct. 3, 1906.
San Antonio Daily Light, Oct. 5, 1906.
San Antonio Daily Light, Aug. 14, 1906.
Galveston Daily News, Nov. 10, 1906.
Galveston Daily News, Sept. 1, 1907.
El Paso Morning News, Feb. 21, 1909.
Daily Leader, April 8, 1909.
Daily Express, Nov. 14, 1909.
Galveston Daily News, Nov. 3, 1910.
New York Times, Jan. 28, 1911.
Findley, Paul B., *The Voice From Way Down East, Radio Broadcasting Station WMAF*. Round Hill Radio Corporation, South Dartmouth Massachusetts, 1923, http://worldradiohistory.com/Archive-Station-Albums/WMAF-Album.pdf.
Shiner Gazette, Dec. 26, 1929.
Maxine Holmes and Gerald D. Saxon, Eds., *The WPA Dallas Guide and History* (Dallas Public Library and Univ. North Texas Press, 1992): 81, https://texashistory.unt.edu/ark:/67531/metadc28336/manifest/.
Jeff Dunn, "Narratives of an Automobile Trip Between Dallas and Fort Worth in 1903," *Legacy, A History Journal for Dallas & North Central Texas*, 27 no. 1 (2015): 40-7.
Rex M. Jim Stever, "Sport Texas PO," *Texas Postal History Society Journal*, 40 no. 3 (2015).
"Electric Gas-Lighter Patent," no. 696108, ark:/67531/metapth508504.
Frank Wagner, "Boll Weevil," *Handbook of Texas Online*, https://www.tshaonline.org/handbook/entries/boll-weevil.
"Seaman A. Knapp,"
https://agrilife.org/southtexas/files/2011/09/0006_SeamanAKnapp.pdf
"Signal Lantern Patent," no. 699576, ark:/67531/metapth510133.

EPILOGUE

San Antonio Daily Light and Gazette, Feb. 12, 1911.

Waxahachie Daily Light, March 29, 1911.

Waxahachie Daily Light, Oct 2, 1911.

San Antonio Daily Light, Feb. 25, 1912.

Libertyville Independent, July 12, 1917.

Bennington Evening News, July 12, 1917.

Abilene Semi Weekly Reporter, July 20, 1917.

Boston Globe, Oct. 14, 1917.

Aransas Pass Progress, Nov. 23, 1917.

Boston Sunday Globe, Aug. 10, 1919.

Boston Sunday Globe, Jan. 19, 1920.

Findley, Paul B., *The Voice From Way Down East, Radio Broadcasting Station WMAF*. Round Hill Radio Corporation, South Dartmouth Massachusetts, 1923, http://worldradiohistory.com/Archive-Station-Albums/WMAF-Album.pdf.

Port Arthur News, Nov. 15, 1936.

Atchison Daily Globe, March 19, 1940.

"Report on Chain Broadcasting," Federal Communications Commission, no. 37-5060, Superintendent of Documents, Washington D.C., May 1941.

Amarillo Globe, Sept. 30, 1941.

Sandusky Register Star News, Feb. 6, 1951.

"Ned Liked to Spend Money," *Life*, Feb. 19, 1951, https://books.google.com/books?id=2EsEAAAAMBAJ&dq=%22Ned+Green%22.

Lewis, Arthur H., *The Day They Shook the Plum Tree* (New York: Harcourt Brace, 1963).

Commerce Journal, Oct. 9, 1975.

Paul Zimmerman, "The Star of Star Island," *Sports Illustrated*, Dec. 13, 1982. https://vault.si.com/vault/1982/12/13/the-star-of-star-island.

Tom Peeler, "Nostalgia, Ned and Mabel," *D Magazine*, December 1984, https://www.dmagazine.com/publications/d-magazine/1984/december/nostalgia-ned-and-mabel/.

Slack, Charles, *Hetty, the Genius and Madness of America's First Female Tycoon* (New York: Harper Collins, 2004).

"Heritage Numismatic Auctions Presents the Gold Rush Collection, Catalog #360," Jan. 12, 2005. https://books.google.com/books?id=Dzwv4olucZEC&pg=PA19.

Doug Wicklund, "A Sea-Going Arsenal: Guns of the Yacht United States," *NRA Museums Senior Curator*, June 12, 2017, https://www.nrablog.com/articles/2017/6/a-sea-going-arsenal-guns-of-the-yacht-united-states/.

"The *Charles W. Morgan*," *National Historical Landmark*, US Dept of Interior National Park Service Document 10-300.

"Coins, Col. Edward Howland Robinson Green," https://coinappraiser

.com/rare-coin-knowledge-center/col-edward-howland-robinson-green/.

"The Collections of Colonel E.H.R. Green," https://www.justcollecting. com/miscellania/the-collections-of-colonel-e-h-r-green.

Forney Historical Preservation League Archives, http://www.historic forney.org/archives/markers.html.

Legal Information Institute, https://www.law.cornell.edu/supreme court/text/306/398.

Paul Freeman, "Abandoned and Little-Known Airfields": Eastern Massachusetts, Round Hill Airport, Round Hill, MA," http://www.airfields -freeman.com/MA/Airfields_MA_SE.htm#roundhill.

Massachusetts Air and Space Museum, Round Hill and Round Hill Airport, http://www.massairspace.org/virtualexhibit/vex12/index.htm.

Carol Mowrey, Isola-Stella: A Unique Craft, Mystic Seaport Museum, http://rosenfeld.musticseaport.org/2018/07/389/.

Round Hill Lab Site, The Center For Land Use Interpretation, https://clui.org/ludb/site/round-hill-lab-site.

"The Witch, the Wench & the Colonel," *William Bryk's Chronicles of Old New York*, https://cityofsmoke.wordpress.com/tag/colonel-e-h-r-green/.

APPENDIX 1
1899 TARPON CLUB MEMBERSHIP BOOK

TARPON CLUB

BY-LAWS
RULES
OFFICERS AND MEMBERS

1899

CLUB HOUSE

SPORT P. O., ARANSAS COUNTY

TEXAS

OFFICERS AND DIRECTORS

1899

PRESIDENT . . . . E. H. R. GREEN
FIRST VICE-PRESIDENT . J. C. VAN BLARCOM
SECOND VICE-PRESIDENT . . A. W. HOUSTON
TREASURER . . . . J. S. LOCKWOOD
SECRETARY . . . . E. M. REARDON

DIRECTORS

J. C. VAN BLARCOM   A. W. HOUSTON
J. S. LOCKWOOD   W. C. CONNOR
              E. H. R. GREEN

3

180

STANDING COMMITTEES

House Committee
W. E. HUGHES
    C. W. OGDEN
            J. T. MASON

Property Committee
J. S. LOCKWOOD
    E. P. WILMOT
            M. B. LOYD

Finance Committee
J. C. VAN BLARCOM
    E. M. REARDON
            E. H. R. GREEN

Rule Committee
ROLLA WELLS
    A. W. HOUSTON
            J. T ESKRIDGE

Library Committee
A. H. BELO
    FRANK HOLLAND
            FRANK GRICE

Membership Committee
HENRY HAMILTON
    ROYAL A. FERRIS
            TYSON S. DINES

Reception Committee
TOM RANDOLPH   J. C. O'CONNOR
A. H. O'NEIL   E. H. TERRELL
SYL. F. SMITH   C. B. KOUNTZE
L. E. LEMAN   S. W. FORDYCE
N. C. CHAPMAN   W. H. LEE

5

181

BY-LAWS

ARTICLE I

OFFICERS—THEIR POWERS AND DUTIES

SECTION 1. The government of the Club shall be entrusted to a Board of Directors, consisting of five members, all of whom shall be elected each year at its annual election, and shall hold their office for one year, and until their successors are elected and qualified.

The officers of the Club shall consist of a President, First and Second Vice-Presidents, Secretary, and Treasurer, who shall be elected by the Board of Directors at their first meeting after each annual election. The officers of the Club shall hold their office for one year, and until their successors are elected and qualified. The President and First and Second Vice-Presidents must be members of the Board of Directors. The Secretary and Treasurer need not be members of the Board of Directors.

Three members of the Board shall constitute a quorum for the transaction of business.

SECTION 2. The President shall preside at meeting of the Club and of the Board and shall be ex-officio member of all committees of the Club. In the absence or disability of the Presi-

7

182

dent, the First Vice-President, and in his absence or disability Second Vice-President, shall perform the duties of the office of President, and, during such time, shall be ex-officio member of all committees of the Club. In their absence a presiding officer may be chosen by ballot.

SECTION 3. The Secretary shall keep a record of the proceedings of the Club, and of the Board, which shall, at all reasonable times be open to the inspection of the members of the Club. He shall notify members of their election; keep a roll of members; issue notices of all meetings of the Club called as hereinafter provided; conduct the correspondence and have the custody of the seal.

SECTION 4. The Treasurer shall collect and disburse the funds. He shall keep the accounts in books belonging to the Club, which shall at all times be open to the inspection of the Board, to whom he shall make monthly reports in writing of the money received and paid out, the amount of funds on hand, and at the annual meeting of the Club make a full report of the receipts and disbursements of the year. He shall also give a bond for the faithful discharge of his duties, with sureties to be approved by the Board.

SECTION 5. The Secretary and the Treasurer, respectively, shall have the power, with the approval of the Board, to employ, at the expense of the Club, such clerical aid as may be necessary in the discharge of their duties.

8

BY-LAWS

SECTION 6. The Board shall control and manage the property of the Club, and the appropriation of its funds, make all contracts and purchases, but shall have no power to make the Club liable for any debt or debts beyond the amount of cash in the hands of the Treasurer or in process of collection.

All committees shall be appointed by the President, subject to the approval of the Board.

It shall be the duty of said Board to prescribe and publish rules regulating the use and occupancy of the rooms of the Club, the care and protection of its property, and defining the powers and duties devolving upon the committees aforesaid.

The Board shall meet for the transaction of business on the first Tuesday of each month, and at any other time when the President or any two members of the Board shall request that such meeting be called. It shall make an annual report of its proceedings to the Club.

SECTION 7. Any officer or director of this Club may be removed from office for cause by a two-thirds vote at any meeting of the Club, notice of such action having been given at a previous meeting; and vacancy in any office may be filled for the remainder of the term by the Board. Neglect of any member of the Board or of any standing committee to attend three consecutive meetings, shall be deemed a tender of his resignation of office, unless a satisfactory explanation shall be given.

9

TARPON CLUB

SECTION 8. All bonds of officials or employes of the Club shall be, at the option of the Board, executed as surety by some responsible Surety Company to be approved by the Board.

ARTICLE II

MEMBERSHIP

SECTION 1. The membership of the Club shall consist of three classes: Members, Honorary Members and Army and Navy Members. Any male citizen of the United States, of lawful age, shall be eligible to membership. All applications for membership shall be signed by the applicant who shall be recommended by at least two members.

All applications for membership shall be referred to and acted upon by the Board, whose proceedings thereon shall be secret, confidential and final. The vote shall be by secret ballot, one negative vote excluding. They shall pass upon each application separately, and at every meeting of the Club report the names of such persons as they have admitted to its membership. No person failing of election shall be again proposed for membership until after the expiration of six months from the time of such action.

10

BY-LAWS

SECTION 2. The names, residence and occupation of persons proposed for membership, with the names of members recommending them, shall be posted on the bulletin board for at least ten days before being acted upon by the Board. No person, although elected to membership, shall be deemed a member until he shall have paid his admission fee. If any person elected shall not, within thirty days after notice of his election shall have been sent to his postoffice address, signify his acceptance and pay his admission fee, together with dues, as indicated in Article III, he shall be deemed to have forfeited his election.

SECTION 3. No officer of the Club shall propose or second any candidate for membership.

SECTION 4. Any person who shall be nominated by a unanimous vote of the Board may be elected an Honorary Member, at a regular meeting of the Club, by a three-fourths vote of the members present at such meeting, and shall enjoy all of the privileges of other members, except voting or holding office.

SECTION 5. Commissioned officers of the Army and Navy, and of the Revenue-Marine and Hospital Service of the United States, not on the retired list, stationed or living in Aransas county or within fifty miles of the Club House may be elected to membership in the manner prescribed for Members, such membership to expire with

11

the removal of members from said district. They shall be exempt from the payment of initiation fee and dues, and shall not be allowed to vote.

The Board shall have power, at their discretion, to admit to the privileges of the Club, upon such terms as they may prescribe, any representative of any foreign nation.

The Board, by unanimous resolution of the members present at any meeting, may extend the privileges of the Club to non-residents of Aransas county for a period of time not exceeding thirty days; such privileges may be extended another thirty days by unanimous vote of those present at any Board meeting.

SECTION 6. Any person who, from any cause, shall cease to be a member, shall forfeit all his rights and interest in the property of the Club.

SECTION 7. The membership of the Club shall be limited to Four Hundred, and shall not be increased beyond that number without a vote of two-thirds of all the members present at any regular meeting of the Club.

SECTION 8. Any member guilty of any misconduct, and especially any member whose conduct shall be hostile to the objects or injurious to the character of this Club, or who shall violate its By-Laws or established rules, may be suspended or expelled from the Club by a two-thirds vote of the Board. No member shall be condemned

12

187

BY-LAWS

without an opportunity to be heard in his defense. The Board shall be the sole judge as to what constitutes misconduct.

ARTICLE III

ADMISSION FEE AND DUES

SECTION 1. The admission fee shall be fifty dollars.

SECTION 2. The annual dues of members shall be fifteen dollars, payable on the first day of September in each year, in advance. Payment of dues by members shall commence with their election, they paying a proportion of the annual dues corresponding to the unexpired portion of the current year, no deduction to be made for fraction of six months.

Resignations will not be received on or after the first day of September unless dues accruing on that day are first paid.

SECTION 3. No member whose dues are unpaid shall be entitled to vote. The Board shall not have power to remit dues. When the dues or other indebtedness of any member shall remain unpaid for two months after proper notice is mailed, his membership is declared forfeited and he shall thereupon cease to be a member of the Club. A member thus

13

188

forfeiting his membership may be reinstated within three months of his forfeiture by the two-thirds vote of the Board, upon payment of all arrears.

ARTICLE IV

VISITORS

Residents within ten miles of the Club House, not members of the Club, shall not be admitted to the Club House, without the consent of the Board, except to the reception room, or to an entertainment given by a member in a private room. A member may invite a stranger, a lady or gentleman, to the use of the Club for a period of two weeks, but can have but one male guest at a time. A member's wife does not require a visitor's card. The invitation may be extended for two weeks upon the written assent of a member of the Board and may be repeated when a gentleman stranger has been absent from the Club for two years and a lady six months. The Board may revoke any such invitation at any time. The names and residences of such strangers and the names of the members introducing them must be recorded, and hosts are held responsible for their guests.

14

BY-LAWS

Any member requesting a card for his private secretary who is actually traveling in that capacity, the Secretary of the Club shall issue the Card good during the member's stay, and same shall not be considered a Visitor's Card. Members shall be responsible for debts contracted by their private secretaries.

ARTICLE V

MEETINGS AND ELECTIONS

SECTION 1. The annual election shall take place on the first Tuesday in September in each year.

Polls shall be opened at twelve o'clock noon and closed at six P. M. The annual meeting of the Club shall be held on the evening of the first Tuesday in September at eight P. M.

SECTION 2. At the regular monthly meeting of the Board in July there shall be appointed a committee of five members of the Club, who shall nominate a ticket for Directors to be voted for at the annual election. The ticket reported by said committee shall be posted on the bulletin board of the Club at least twenty days before election. Any number of members, not less than ten, may nominate other candidates for Directors. Such nomination shall be in writing, with the signatures of the persons so nominating,

15

and be placed in the hands of the Secretary. A certificate of the Secretary shall be appended to the names which shall be nominated, other than those nominated by the regular Nominating Committee, certifying that they have been nominated by not less than ten members of the Club; but the names of all persons to be voted for at said election shall be posted on the bulletin board at least fifteen days before election. When the time has expired in which the names of candidates may be posted, the Board shall cause the names of all legally posted candidates to be printed on one ticket, alphabetically arranged, and the ticket so made up shall, together with a printed copy of Sections 1 and 2, Article 5 of By-Laws, be mailed to each member at least ten days before election. No other form of ticket than the one hereinbefore provided shall be used on the day of election, and no member shall mail any other member any other form of ticket, or any ticket of regular form on which the names of any particular candidates are marked, nor shall any such marked or other ticket be urged upon members upon the floor of the Club House upon the day of election. Each member voting, so far as he desires to exercise the privilege, shall place a check mark opposite the name of the five candidates of his choice, and only names so checked shall be counted by the Judges of Election. A member may vote by sending his ballot, over his own signature, to the Judges of Election. Proxies sent to others than

16

191

the Judges of Election will not be considered. The names of successful candidates shall be posted on the bulletin board when the result is determined.

SECTION 3. In addition to the annual meeting there shall be meetings of the Club for the transaction of business on the first Tuesdays in June and December at eight o'clock P. M.

SECTION 4. Special meetings of the Club may be called at any time by order of the President, or by request of two members of the Board. Ten members may call a special meeting, with or without the consent of the officers, by filing with the Secretary, for posting, a written call over their own signatures. The call for a special meeting shall set forth the purpose of the meeting, and notice thereof shall be mailed to each member ten days prior to the time of such meeting, and no business other than that specified in the call and notice, shall be transacted.

SECTION 5. The fiscal year shall commence with the first day of September each year.

17

192

TARPON CLUB

ARTICLE VI

RULES OF PROCEDURE

SECTION 1. The regular order of business at all meetings of the Club shall be as follows:

1. Reading of the minutes of the last meeting.

2. Report of Standing Committees.

3. Report of Special Committees.

4. General business.

But this order may be changed by order of the Club.

SECTION 2. Robert's Rules of Order shall govern the meetings of the Club, when not inconsistent with these By-Laws.

SECTION 3. Twenty members or proxies shall constitute a quorum at all meetings of the Club.

SECTION 4. All committees shall be appointed by the presiding officer.

SECTION 5. No member shall be permitted to speak more than once upon the same subject, nor more than ten minutes at a time, without the unanimous consent of the Club.

SECTION 6. All elections shall be by ballot.

18

BY-LAWS

Section 7. Any motion or resolution offered for the consideration of the Club, shall, at the request of any member, be reduced to writing before it is acted upon.

Section 8. All resolutions, except those presented by the Board, or Committee of the Club, or by petition of fifteen members of the Club at the request of any three members present, shall be referred to an appropriate committee before action thereon by the Club.

ARTICLE VII

AMENDMENT OF BY-LAWS

Section 1. Any By-Law may be amended or new By-Law adopted by a vote of two-thirds of the members present or proxies, at any regular meeting of the Club, provided the same shall have been proposed in writing at a previous meeting, and written notice thereof shall have been mailed to each member of the Club at least ten days prior to the meeting at which such question shall be presented for action, and the same shall have been posted on the bulletin board at least ten days prior to such meeting.

19

HOUSE RULES

1. The Club House will be open to members every day in the year.

2. The wine room shall be closed at 2 A. M., and on Sunday at 11 o'clock P. M., except when otherwise especially ordered by the House Committee.

3. Residents within ten miles of the Club House, not members of the Club, shall not be admitted to the Club House without the consent of the Board, except to the reception room, or to an entertainment given by a member in a private room.

A member may, subject to the foregoing provision, personally introduce one visitor to the privileges of the Club for one day, by recording the name of such visitor in the visitor's register.

Upon written application of a member a card may be issued by the Secretary admitting a visitor, not residing within ten miles of the Club House, to the privileges of the Club House for a period of two weeks, and such card may, on the written consent of a member of the Board, be extended for a further period of two weeks; provided, however, that no member can have more than one male guest at a time. No such card shall subsequently be issued to any such non-resident, until he shall have been absent from the Club for a period of not less than two years from the expiration of the last card issued to him hereunder.

The Board may revoke any such card at any time. The name and residence of each visitor, and the names of members introducing them, must be recorded.

4. A member recommending or introducing a visitor shall be responsible for the conduct of such visitor, and for any debt or liability incurred by him.

5. No guest shall give an entertainment in the Club House without the consent of the House Committee.

6. The main dining room shall not be given up to the use of any club, society or persons not members of the Club.

7. Private dining rooms shall not be assigned to parties numbering less than three persons, and reasonable notice of any entertainment must be given at the office.

Members who desire to entertain in private dining rooms, when the party includes more than five persons who are not members, shall first obtain the consent of the House Committee.

. 8. No member shall be allowed to use a private dining room for more than two consecutive days without the consent of the House Committee.

22

9. For the purpose of calling attention of members to any indebtedness notice shall be mailed every Monday. On the second Monday thereafter the names of delinquents, with the amounts due, shall be posted on the bulletin board. If payment shall not be made within one week from date of posting, further credit to such member shall cease.

10. The annual dues shall be payable September first of each year. On the first day of the month following, the names of delinquents, with the amounts due, shall be posted in the office of the Club.

11. The right of members to occupy sleeping rooms in the Club House may be terminated at any time by the Board.

12. No member, guest or visitor shall give money or other gratuity to any servant of the Club, and any member so doing shall be deemed guilty of a misdemeanor and shall be dealt with as provided in the By-Laws. Any servant receiving a gratuity from any member or guest shall be dismissed.

13. No member shall take from the Club House any article belonging to the Club, nor from the library or reading room any book, pamphlet or newspaper, nor mutilate or destroy same.

23

14. Servants shall not be sent out of the Club House. Upon application at the office a messenger will be summoned.

15. No subscriptions shall be solicited, nor any article exposed for sale, nor any advertising permitted in the Club House, except the usual holiday subscription for the employes of the Club.

16. No refreshments shall be sent out of the Club House.

17. Smoking shall not be permitted in the main dining room except at banquets.

18. Dogs will not be permitted in the Club House.

19. Members are required to make all suggestions or complaints in writing and deposit same in the recommendation box provided for that purpose in the office. Complaints addressed personally to members of the Board will not receive attention.

20. It shall be the duty of every member of the Club to report in writing any violation of the rules to the Secretary, who shall make a report thereof to the Board.

21. Upon the written application of a member, a card may be issued by the Secretary for use by a lady which shall admit her to the privileges of the Club when accompanied by a member or by a member's wife.

24

HOUSE RULES

22. The names of all lady visitors shall be registered in a book kept for that purpose, together with the name of the member introducing them, or whose name appears on the admission card presented.

23. No member shall be entitled to have more than one lady's card issued at one time, nor have a card issued while one issued upon his application is outstanding.

25

199

COMMITTEES

COMMITTEES ESTABLISHED BY THE BOARD OF

DIRECTORS—THEIR POWERS AND DUTIES

A House Committee of three which shall direct and control the various departments of the house; shall purchase the supplies necessary for consumption, and shall have immediate supervision of all employes, except office employes.

A Property Committee of three which shall have charge of the building occupied by the Club and the care of the same; shall see to insurance, taxes, preservation and renewal of all property of the Club, including the furniture, and shall attend to the purchase of all articles needed by the Club having a permanent nature.

A Finance Committee of three which shall have the general supervision of all the financial affairs of the Club.

A Rules Committee of three which shall enforce the Rules for the preservation of order in the house, and shall have charge of all matters pertaining to the conduct of the members.

A Library Committee of three who shall have charge of the Library, all books and periodicals, with authority to expend such sums of money

27

200

upon the same as may be voted therefor by the Board, or procured by voluntary contributions.

A Membership Committee of three which shall examine and report upon all applications for membership.

A Reception Committee of ten which shall have charge, under the direction of the Board, of all receptions, banquets and social functions given by the Club.

28

201

MEMBERS

Adams, W. A.	Saint Louis, Missouri
Ainsworth, D. H.	San Antonio, Texas
Aldridge, G. N.	Dallas, Texas
Allen, W. P.	Terrell, Texas
Alexander, C. H.	Dallas, Texas
Allen, A. A.	Saint Louis, Missouri
Allyn, Chas. H.	Corsicana, Texas
Armstrong, J. S.	Dallas, Texas
Arnold, Frank,	San Antonio, Texas
Ashton, L.	Dallas, Texas
Aubrey, Wm.	San Antonio, Texas
Badger, F. J.	San Antonio, Texas
Baker, J. A., Jr.	Houston, Texas
Baldwin, B. B. Jr.	Paris, Texas
Barnhart, G. W.	Saint Louis, Missouri
Beddoe, T. D.	Ontario, Canada
Beilharz, T.	Dallas, Texas
Bell, T. C.	San Antonio, Texas
Bell, Jas. H.	San Antonio, Texas
Belo, A. H.	Dallas, Texas
Bergstrom, Oscar	San Antonio, Texas
Bewley, M. P.	Fort Worth, Texas
Bissell, J. B.	Denver, Colorado
Black, H. C.	Waco, Texas
Blackford, G. L.	Denison, Texas

31

202

TARPON CLUB

Blake, J. W.   Mexia, Texas
Blossom, H. A.   Saint Louis, Missouri
Bolles, R. J.   Colorado Springs, Colorado
Bonner, W. A.   Dallas, Texas
Booth, C. H.   Taylor, Texas
Boren, B. N.   Dallas, Texas
Boyce, W. D.   Chicago, Illinois
Brackenridge, G. W.   San Antonio, Texas
Brenizer, N. O.   Austin, Texas
Bryant, W. H.   Denver, Colorado
Brown, J. G.   Austin, Texas
Bryant, W. G.   Denver, Colorado
Burkett, G. W.   Palestine, Texas
Buck, J. W.   Saint Louis, Missouri
Buchanan, Wm.   Texarkana, Texas

Calhoun, D. R.   Saint Louis, Missouri
Cameron, Wm.   Waco, Texas
Camp, T. L.   Dallas, Texas
Cary, A. P.   Dallas, Texas
Carlin, P. V.   Denver, Colorado
Carlton, O. S.   Dallas, Texas
Cartwright, M.   Terrell, Texas
Carver, E. B.   Henrietta, Texas
Casey, Martin   Fort Worth, Texas
Cate, H. M.   Mineola, Texas
Chandler, E. B.   San Antonio, Texas
Chapman, N. C.   Saint Louis, Missouri
Cheerer, J. D.   New York, New York
Chisholm, S. H.   New York, New York
Clifford, G. G.   San Antonio, Texas
Cobb, C. S.   Denison, Texas

32

203

MEMBERS

Cobbs, T. D.	San Antonio, Texas
Cochran, Sam P.	Dallas, Texas
Cochran, A. G.	Saint Louis, Missouri
Cochran, T. B.	Austin, Texas
Coke, H. C.	Dallas, Texas
Connor, W. C.	Dallas, Texas
Connor, W. O.	Dallas, Texas
Conway, J. C.	Cleburne, Texas
Cook, Hamilton,	Dallas, Texas
Corcoran, J. W.	Pine Bluff, Arkansas
Corley, T. E.	Terrell, Texas
Craney, J. W.	Terrell, Texas
Cravens, J. R.	Dallas, Texas
Crawford, J. D.	Marshall, Texas
Crawford, G. L.	Saint Louis, Missouri
Craycroft, H. A.	Dallas, Texas
Crush, W. G.	Dallas, Texas
Dargan, V. C.	Dallas, Texas
Davis, J. T.	Waco, Texas
Dawley, C. W.	Dallas, Texas
Deere, C. H.	Moline, Illinois
Dillon, M.	El Paso, Texas
Dines, T. S.	Denver, Colorado
Dodd, S. M.	Saint Louis, Missouri
Downman, R. H.	Waco, Texas
Downs, F. F.	Temple, Texas
Drummond, H. I.	Saint Louis, Missouri
Duke, J. C.	Dallas, Texas
Earnest, D. C.	Dallas, Texas
Edson, J. A.	Tyler, Texas

33

Edwards, G. L.	Saint Louis, Missouri
Eichlitz, G. C.	San Antonio, Texas
Elmendorf, W. S.	Aspen, Colorado
Ellwood, I. L.	DeKalb, Illinois
Enders, Wm.	Saint Louis, Missouri
Eppstein, M. L.	Denison, Texas
Eppstein, M.	Dallas, Texas
Eskridge, J. T.	Denver, Colorado
Euston, Alex	Saint Louis, Missouri
Evans, I. H.	Austin, Texas
Everett, Sylvester	Cleveland, Ohio
Ferris, R. A.	Dallas, Texas
Fascue, P. H.	Sulphur Springs, Texas
Faulkner, A.	Alsdorf, Texas
Finley, S. M.	Dallas, Texas
Fleming, Fred	Corsicana, Texas
Fordyce, S. W.	Saint Louis, Missouri
Fort, W. V.	Waco, Texas
Forwood, Reginald	Paris, Texas
Francis, D. R.	Saint Louis, Missouri
Franklin, T. H.	San Antonio, Texas
French, A	Pittsburg, Pennsylvania
Fry, E. J.	Marshall, Texas
Gaines, R. R.	Austin, Texas
Galbraith, R. M.	Pine Bluff, Arkansas
Garitty, James	Corsicana, Texas
Garrison, D. E.	Saint Louis, Missouri
Gaston, Wm. H.	Dallas, Texas
Gates, J. W.	New York, New York
George, J. M.	San Antonio, Texas

34

205

MEMBERS

Gilmore, S. J.	Denver, Colorado
Glidden, C. J.	Lowell, Massachusetts
Glogau, Emile	Saint Louis, Missouri
Godley, R. B.	Dallas, Texas
Gordon, Jack	Paris, Texas
Gould, Edwin	New York, New York
Graham, B. B.	Saint Louis, Missouri
Grant, J. B.	Denver, Colorado
Grant, John	Paris, Texas
Gratz, Benj.	Saint Louis, Missouri
Graves, Amos	San Antonio, Texas
Green, E. H. R.	Terrell, Texas
Green, G. H.	Dallas, Texas
Grice, Frank	San Antonio, Texas
Grigsby, G. M. D.	Jefferson, Texas
Grinnan, J. S.	Terrell, Texas
Haarstick, Wm. T.	Saint Louis, Missouri
Hall, W. L.	Dallas, Texas
Hall, Kirk	Dallas, Texas
Hallett, M.	Denver, Colorado
Hamilton, Henry	Dallas, Texas
Hamilton, H. E.	Dallas, Texas
Hamilton, C. H.	Waco, Texas
Hammond, F. M.	Lancaster, Texas
Hampton, J. W.	Abilene, Texas
Handlan, A. H.	Saint Louis, Missouri
Hardwick, W. P.	Fort Worth, Texas
Hare, Silas, Jr.	Sherman, Texas
Harrington, C. E.	Denver, Colorado
Harris, John	Terrell, Texas
Harrison, W. B.	Fort Worth, Texas

35

206

TARPON CLUB

Harry, D. W. C.	Dallas, Texas
Harry, T. C.	Dallas, Texas
Hart, E. A.	Cincinnati, Ohio
Haynes, J. J.	Laredo, Texas
Heard, Bryan	Houston, Texas
Heath, P. S.	Washington, D. C.
Hefley, W. T.	Cameron, Texas
Higgins, C. C.	Bastrop, Texas
Hodgman, C.	Saint Louis, Missouri
Hogg, J. S.	Austin, Texas
Holland, Frank	Dallas, Texas
Hollins, H. B.	New York, New York
Hopkins, James	Saint Louis, Missouri
Hornby, John	Fort Worth, Texas
House, T. W.	Houston, Texas
Houston, A. W.	San Antonio, Texas
Houston, Reagan	San Antonio, Texas
Hoxie, G. H.	Chicago, Illinois
Hughes, C. J.	Denver, Colorado
Hughes, W. E.	Dallas, Texas
Hugo, Charles	San Antonio, Texas
Hunter, R. D.	Fort Worth, Texas
Huntington, C. P.	New York, New York
James, Harry C.	Denver, Colorado
Johnson, J. R.	Austin, Texas
Jones, B.	Saint Louis, Missouri
Jones, J. H.	Houston, Texas
Kampman, H. D.	San Antonio, Texas
Keating, C. A.	Dallas, Texas
Kenedy, John	Alice, Texas

36

207

MEMBERS

Kenna, E. D.	Chicago, Illinois
Kerens, R. C.	Saint Louis, Missouri
Kleberg, R. J.	Corpus Christi, Texas
Knight, H. F.	Saint Louis, Missouri
Koëhler, Otto	San Antonio, Texas
Kokernot, J. W.	San Antonio, Texas
Kountze, C. B.	Denver, Colorado
Lasater, E. C.	San Antonio, Texas
Lee, W. H.	Saint Louis, Missouri
Leith, J. E.	Terrell, Texas
Leman, L. E.	Denver, Colorado
Lewis, H. C.	Saint Louis, Missouri
Lewis, P. J.	San Antonio, Texas
Lindsay, J. M.	Gainesville, Texas
Lindsay, L. B.	Gainesville, Texas
Lionberger, I. H.	Saint Louis, Missouri
Lockwood, J. S.	San Antonio, Texas
Lowry, R. J.	Atlanta, Georgia
Loyd, M. B.	Fort Worth, Texas
Lucas, J. B. C.	Saint Louis, Missouri
Lyon, C. A.	Sherman, Texas
McCampbell, Atlee	Corpus Christi, Texas
McDonald, B. P.	Waco, Texas
McElhone, F. H.	Dallas, Texas
McEntire, W. R.	Dallas, Texas
McGown, Floyd	San Antonio, Texas
McGrath, Wm. H.	Dallas, Texas
McHenry, Estell	Saint Louis, Missouri
McLemore, Jeff	Austin, Texas
McLendon, J. S.	Waco, Texas

37

McMillan, W. N.	Saint Louis, Missouri
McNaught, F. H.	Denver, Colorado
Madill, G. A.	Saint Louis, Missouri
Mallam, G. H.	Beaumont, Texas
Mallinckrodt, Edw.	Saint Louis, Missouri
Marshall, F. E.	Saint Louis, Missouri
Martin, E. J.	San Antonio, Texas
Martin, W. B.	Terrell, Texas
Mason, J. T.	Denver, Colorado
Maxwell, J. W.	Dallas, Texas
Meade, G. P.	Fort Worth, Texas
Merchant, G. W.	Dallas, Texas
Miller, D.	Saint Paul, Minnesota
Miller, Jeff	Houston, Texas
Milroy, A. D.	Brenham, Texas
Mims, S.	Fort Worth, Texas
Minor, B. B., Jr.	Brenham, Texas
Monserrate, M. D.	San Antonio, Texas
Morse, C. S.	Austin, Texas
Morton, J. W.	Saint Louis, Missouri
Moss, S. E.	Cleburne, Texas
Munson, J. T.	Denison, Texas
Munson, W. B.	Denison, Texas
Murray, O. G.	Baltimore, Maryland
Neidringhaus, T. K.	Saint Louis, Missouri
Newby, W. G.	Fort Worth, Texas
Newell, O. S.	San Antonio, Texas
Nunn, W. G.	Ladonia, Texas
O'Brien, Wm.	Aspen, Colorado
O'Connor, J. C.	Dallas, Texas

38

209

MEMBERS

O'Neil, A. H.	Paris, Texas
Ogden, C. W.	San Antonio, Texas
Oliver, R.	Groesbeck, Texas
Oppenheimer, D. G.	Dallas, Texas
Paramore, F. W.	Saint Louis, Missouri
Parker, J. W.	Taylor, Texas
Patterson, W. H.	New York, New York
Peeler, J. L.	Austin, Texas
Perin, Clifford	Cincinnati, Ohio
Perin, F. L.	Cincinnati, Ohio
Peters, T. E.	Colorado Springs, Colorado
Pierce, H. C.	Saint Louis, Missouri
Pillot, C. G.	Houston, Texas
Polk, L. J.	Galveston, Texas
Poor, H. W.	New York, New York
Potter, R. E.	Dallas, Texas
Priest, H. S.	Saint Louis, Missouri
Quinlan, G. A.	Houston, Texas
Randolph, Tom	Sherman, Texas
Reardon, E. M.	Dallas, Texas
Reynolds, W. E.	Albany, Texas
Reynolds, G. T.	Albany, Texas
Reynolds, W. E.	Denver, Colorado
Richardson, J. C.	Saint Louis, Missouri
Ridgeway, A. C.	Florence, Colorado
Ripley, Dan	Galveston, Texas
Roberts, M. C.	Terrell, Texas
Robertson, J. H.	Austin, Texas
Robins, M. L.	Houston, Texas
Robinson, D. B.	Saint Louis, Missouri

39

TARPON CLUB

Ross, T. D.	Fort Worth, Texas
Rotan, Edward	Waco, Texas
Rouse, H. C.	New York, New York
Sanders, J. F.	Denver, Colorado
Sanger, Alex	Dallas, Texas
Sawyer, W. E.	LaCrosse, Wisconsin
Schneider, J. E.	Dallas, Texas
Schofield, J. D.	Dallas, Texas
Scott, H. C.	Saint Louis, Missouri
Seeger, J. B.	Dallas, Texas
Seley, W. W.	Waco, Texas
Senn, Nicholas	Chicago, Illinois
Simpson, J. N.	Dallas, Texas
Skinner, G. W.	Denver, Colorado
Smith, S. F.	Denver, Colorado
Snider, A. J.	Kansas City, Missouri
Snyder, R. M.	Kansas City, Missouri
Soper, A. W.	New York, New York
Speer, H. F.	Dallas, Texas
Spenser, J. W.	Fort Worth, Texas
Staacke, H. G.	San Antonio, Texas
Stevens, J. J.	San Antonio, Texas
Stevens, G. A.	Moline, Illinois
Stewart, D. A.	Dallas, Texas
Stillman, T. E.	New York, New York
Sugg, E. C.	Sugden, Indian Territory
Sullivan, D. J.	San Antonio, Texas
Sullivan, W. C.	San Antonio, Texas
Swenson, E. P.	New York, New York
Swenson, S. A.	New York, New York
Swope, Joseph	Dallas, Texas

40

211

MEMBERS

Terrell, E. H.	San Antonio, Texas
Thatcher, J. A.	Denver, Colorado
Thompson, C. A.	Saint Louis, Missouri
Thompson, Wm.	Dallas, Texas
Thompson, W. B.	Saint Louis, Missouri
Tips, Walter	Austin, Texas
Townsend, W. J.	Dallas, Texas
Trezevant, J. T.	Dallas, Texas
Tullock, A. J.	Leavenworth, Kansas
Turner, W. G.	Fort Worth, Texas
Van Blarcom, J. C.	Saint Louis, Missouri
Wahrmund, Otto	San Antonio, Texas
Walsh, E., Jr.	Saint Louis, Missouri
Ward, R. H.	Fort Worth, Texas
Warner, S. G.	Tyler, Texas
Webb, Sam	Albany, Texas
Wells, James	Dallas, Texas
Wells, Rolla	Saint Louis, Missouri
Welton, L. M.	San Antonio, Texas
Wentz, D. B.	Saint Louis, Missouri
West, T. F.	Fort Worth, Texas
Whitney, A. R.	New York, New York
Whitaker, Edward	Saint Louis, Missouri
Whiteselle, J. E.	Corsicana, Texas
Wickes, T. H.	Chicago, Illinois
Williams, G. H.	Paris, Texas
Wilmot, E. P.	Austin, Texas
Winchell, B. L.	Denver, Colorado
Wolf, H. O.	Dallas, Texas

41

TARPON CLUB

Wood, S. N.   Denver, Colorado
Wood, H. E.   Denver, Colorado
Woodward, W. H.   Saint Louis, Missouri
Wortham, L. J.   Austin, Texas
Wright, Geo. M.   Saint Louis, Missouri

Yoakum, B. F.   Saint Louis, Missouri

Zang, J. F.   Dallas, Texas

42

213

IN MEMORIAM

WILLIAM CAMERON

APPENDIX 2

MEMBERS

There were 334 names listed in the original 1899 Tarpon Club membership book (Appendix 1). As would be expected, the membership was fluid – members died or quit, and new ones were added. The following is a list of the original member names showing their residence cities, professions, and other miscellaneous information. It is by no means exhaustive but is interesting as it sheds light on the occupations and some notable achievements of E.H.R.'s exceptional sportsmen at the turn of the 20th century.

Name	Residence city	Occupation, etc.

Adams, W.A.   St. Louis, MO   Physician; Active in
Republican party; Fished tarpon at Aransas Pass as early as 1896.
Ainsworth, D.H.   San Antonio, TX   Attorney; Family
active in San Antonio society.
Aldredge, George N.   Dallas, TX   Director of National
Exchange Bank of Dallas; Chairman of Cotton Growers of Texas (early
1900s); Govt. liaison for boll weevil studies; NOTE: Original 1899 club
membership book spelling was ALDRIDGE.
Allen, A.A.   Dallas, TX   General Manager of
Missouri, Kansas & Texas Railroad Co.; NOTE: City listed incorrectly in
1899 club membership book.
Allen, Walter P.   Terrell, TX   Banker; Had a 40-
year friendship with E.H.R. Green.
Alexander, C.H.   Dallas, TX   President of Electric
Street Railway.
Allyn, Charles H.   Corsicana, TX   Capitalist; Corsicana
mayor; Director of Texas Petroleum Association; Used title of "Captain."
Armstrong, J.S.   Dallas, TX   Dallas Packery
owner.
Arnold, Frank   San Antonio, TX   President of Lone
Star Brewery; Chairman of Texas Travelers Protective Assoc.; Director of
San Antonio World's Fair poultry and fish exhibit; Spanish War veteran
with the rank of Colonel.
Ashton, L.   Dallas, TX   Physician
Aubrey, William   San Antonio, TX   Attorney; President
of San Antonio Bar Assoc.; Active in San Antonio YMCA; Member of
San Antonio Democratic Club.

Badger, F.J.   San Antonio, TX   Major; Inspector of
Texas Volunteer Guard; Member of San Antonio Democratic Club.
Baker, J.A. Jr. (Capt.)   Houston, TX   Attorney; Banker;
Member of Eagle Lake Rod & Gun Club.
Baldwin, B.B. Jr.   Paris, TX   Contractor
Barnhart, G.W.   St. Louis, MO   Real Estate;
minerals.
Beddoe, T.D.   Ontario, Canada   Representative for
Hiram Walker & Sons syndicate.
Beilharz, Theodore   Dallas, TX   Contractor
Bell, Thad C.   San Antonio, TX   Insurance; Member
1896 Republican Executive Committee; 1898 and 1904 Republican
Convention delegate.

Bell, J.H.   San Antonio, TX   Physician; 1904
Republican Convention delegate.
Belo, A.H.   Dallas, TX   Insurance; Ranching
Bergstrom, Oscar   San Antonio, TX   President of Dyna-
Neutron Co.; Invented process for generating electricity from fuel; Patent
for molding pipe.
Bewley, M.P.   Fort Worth, TX   Insurance; Director
Fort Worth market center.
Bissell, J.B.   Denver, CO   Attorney
Black, H.C.   Waco, TX   Physician; Active in
Masons.
Blackford, G.L.   Denison, TX   President of Denison
State National Bank; Director Dennison, Bonham & New Orleans
Railroad; Arrested in 1896 after a duel with H.P. Kinsey.
Blake, J.W.   Mexía, TX   Attorney; Chairman
of 1898 Democratic Convention.
Blossom, H.A.   St. Louis, MO   President of Missouri
Assoc. of Fire Insurance Agents.
Bolles, R.J.   Colorado Springs, CO   Principal in H.A.
Riedell Investment Co.; President of Juniata Co.
Bonner, W.A.   Dallas, TX   Real estate; Banking
Booth, C.H.   Taylor, TX   Director of Taylor
National Bank; President of Taylor Livestock and Fair Association.
Boren, B.N.   Dallas, TX   Merchant;
Confederate veteran – rank of Captain; Died in 1903.
Boyce, W.D.   Chicago, IL   Owner of W.D.
Boyce Publishing Co., *Chicago Ledger*, and Boyce Building; Big game
hunter with East Africa safaris; 1896 Republican congressional candidate;
Credited as "Father of the Boy Scouts."
Brackenridge, G.W.   San Antonio, TX   President of Alamo
National Bank; Dallas Fire Commissioner; Member of state university
board of regents; President of San Antonio Water Works Co.; Co-owner of
sugar and paper mill in Sugar Land; 1904 Republican Convention delegate.
Brenizer, N.O.   Austin, TX   Surgeon
Brown, J.G.   Austin, TX   Banker
Bryant, W.G.   Denver, CO   Principal at Dorbin
Mining Co., and Webb City-Carterville Foundry & Machine Works; Also,
resident of Carterville, Missouri.
Bryant, W.H.   Denver, CO   Attorney
Burkett, G.W.   Palestine, TX   Attorney; 1900
Republican State Committee member and candidate for governor.
Buck, J. Whitworth   St. Louis, MO   Principal of
Farmington Telephone Co.
Buchanan, William   Texarkana, TX   Merchant

217

Calhoun, D.R.   St. Louis, MO   President of Ely &
Walker Dry Goods; NOTE: City and state listed incorrectly in original club
membership book.

Cameron, William   Waco, TX   Lumber; Died in
1899; NOTE: City listed incorrectly in original club membership book.

Camp, T.L.   Dallas, TX   Judge; Leader in
state Democratic party.

Cary, Arthur P.   Dallas, TX   Businessman; Died
in 1901 of pneumonia 3 hours after his 7-year-old son drowned.

Carlin, P.V.   Denver, CO   Physician; Denver
Board of Education.

Carlton, O.S.   Dallas, TX   State agent for
American Union Life Insurance.

Cartwright, M.   Terrell, TX   Cattle

Carver, E.B.   Henriette, TX   President of Gulf &
Brazos Valley Railroad; Cattleman.

Casey, Martin   Fort Worth, TX   Railroad Investor;
Honorary title of Colonel; Chairman of the Accidental Bivalve Club.

Cate, H.M.   Mineola, TX   Grocer

Chandler, E.B.   San Antonio, TX   President of
Chandler Loan and Trust Co.; President San Antonio Golf Club.

Chapman, Nelson C.   St. Louis, MO   Capitalist; President
of Eau Claire Lumber Co.; President of Harvard Club.

Cheerer, J.D.   New York, NY   Capitalist; Principal
of Potter-Lovell Co.; Member Rockaway Polo Club and New York City
Yacht Club.

Chisholm, S.H.   New York, NY   President of
American Grass Twine Co.; Vice Pres. Cleveland Rolling Mill Co.

Clifford, G.G.   San Antonio, TX   San Antonio
postmaster; Member 1896 Republican Executive Committee; 1898 and
1904 Republican Convention delegate.

Cobb, C.S.   Denison TX   Director of Sherman,
Shreveport & Southern Railway, Leader of Lily Whites in 1896.

Cobbs, T.D.   San Antonio, TX   Attorney

Cochran, A.G.   St. Louis, MO   General Solicitor of
Missouri Pacific Railway.

Cochran, Sam P.   Dallas, TX   Director of
Trezevant & Cochran Insurance; Director at SW Life Insurance Co.;
Member of Dallas Commercial Club; High ranking Mason.

Cochran, T.B.   Austin, TX   Attorney; Judge;
Principal of Dallas Freight Bureau.

Coke, Henry C.   Dallas, TX   Attorney; Director of
National Exchange Bank of Dallas; Son drowned in 1900.

Connor, W.C. Dallas, TX President of Dallas Terminal Railroad & Union Depot Co.; Dallas Mayor; Director of National Exchange Bank of Dallas; 1898 Tarpon Club Board of Directors.

Connor, W.O. Dallas, TX Director of Dallas Terminal Railroad & Union Depot Co.

Conway, J.C. Cleburne, TX Principal of Conway & Leeper Lumber Co.

Cook, Hamilton Dallas, TX Agency inspector for NY Life Insurance Co.

Corcoran, J.W. Pine Bluff, AR Businessman

Corley, Thomas E. Terrell, TX Treasurer of Texas Midland Railroad.

Craney, J.W. Terrell, TX Contractor; Rock Island Railway; Also, resident of Kansas City.

Cravens, J.R. Dallas, TX Agent for S.D. Sudder Fire Insurance.

Crawford, G.L. St. Louis, MO Banking; Invested in racehorses and greyhounds; Owned a yacht in Newport Rhode Island.

Crawford, J.D. Marshall, TX President and Director of Commerce National Bank.

Craycroft, Hunter A. Dallas, TX Insurance; Involved in boll weevil research.

Crush, W.G. Dallas, TX Passenger agent and Director of Missouri, Kansas & Texas Railway; Staged the infamous "Crash at Crush" on September 15, 1896.

Dargan, V.C. Dallas, TX Attorney; Drafted by-laws for the Texas State Sportsmen's Association.

Davis, J.T. Waco, TX Principal of Waco Loan Agency; Owned a farm south of Waco.

Dawley, C.W. Dallas, TX Vice President of Anheuser-Busch Brewing Co.; Director, Texas Coal Co.; Vice President of Cavanal Coal and Mining Co; Held 1899 record club tarpon catch mounted on the club wall; Held a compressor patent.

Deere, Charles H. Moline, IL President of John Deere Manufacturing; Active in state and national Republican party.

Dillon, M. El Paso, TX Customs Collector; Civil War veteran; Involved in 1898 state Republican primaries.

Dines, Tyson S. Denver, CO Attorney

Dodd, S.M. St. Louis, MO Vice President of American Central Insurance Co.; Director of 1904 St. Louis World's Fair.

Downman, Robert H. Waco, TX Minerals; Owner of R.H. Downman Lumber Co.; Principal at Wm. Cameron & Co.

Downs, F.F. Temple, TX President of First National Bank of Temple.

Drummond, H.I. St. Louis, MO Banking; Director of 1904 St. Louis World's Fair.

Duke, J.C. Dallas, TX Banking; Vice President of First National Bank of Frost.

Earnest, D.C. Dallas, TX President of Texas Short Line Co.; Owner Consumers Lignite Co. and Lone Star Salt Works.

Edson, J.A. Tyler, TX General Manager of Kansas City Southern Railway Co.; Director of St. Louis & Southwestern Railway.

Edwards, G.L. St. Louis, MO President of A.G. Edwards & Sons Brokerage Co.

Eichlitz, George C. San Antonio, TX Insurance; Principal of Geo. C. Eichlitz & Co., Director San Antonio Baseball Assoc.

Elmendorf, W.S. Aspen, CO Attorney; Member Jamaica Rod and Rifle Association.

Ellwood, Isaac L. DeKalb, IL Principal in American Steel & Wire Co.; Honorary Colonel; Barbed wire pioneer; Texas rancher.

Enders, Wm. St. Louis, MO Principal at William Enders Stove Co.

Eppstein, M.L. Denison, TX Liquor distributor

Eppstein, Max Dallas, TX Principal of Dallas Brewery.

Eskridge, J.T. Denver, CO Physician; Board of Trustees Colorado State Medical Society.

Euston, Alexander St. Louis, MO President of National Linseed Co.; Director of American Shot Association; Inventor who patented hydraulic press for extracting oil.

Evans, I.H. Austin, TX Real Estate; Military major.

Everett, Sylvester Cleveland, OH Attorney; Ousted as 1899 Republic National Convention delegate by Mark Hanna; NOTE: Named spelled differently in 1899 club membership book.

Fascue, P.H. Sulphur Springs, TX Principal of Sulphur Springs First National Bank.

Faulkner, Alsdorf (Andy) Alsdorf, TX Passenger Agent for Houston & Texas Central Railroad; Civil War veteran; Colonel in state militia; NOTE: Named spelled differently in 1899 club membership book.

220

Ferris, Royal A.   Dallas, TX   President of National Exchange Bank; Vice President of 1904 Texas State Fair committee.

Finley, S.M.   Dallas, TX   Principal of Dallas Mortgage & Loan Co.

Fleming, Fred   Corsicana, TX   President of Western Bank & Trust Co.

Fordyce, S.W.   St. Louis, MO   Capitalist; Director of St. Louis, Brownsville & Mexico Railroad; Director of Kansas City Southern Railway; Director of St. Louis Union Trust Co.; Receiver of Stuttgart & Arkansas River Railroad; Later founded Point Isabel Fishing & Hunting Club; Active in Democratic politics.

Fort, W.V.   Waco, TX   Insurance; Director of Texas Central Railroad.

Forwood, Reginald   Paris, TX   Manufacturer; Inventor who held patents on a railroad car fender, mailbox signal.

Francis, David R.   St. Louis, MO   Missouri Governor; President of 1904 World's Fair; Vice Pres. of Merchants-Laclede National Bank.

Franklin, T.H.   San Antonio, TX   Attorney; Military major; Member Houston Light Guard.

French, A.   Pittsburgh, PA   Principal in French Steel Works.

Fry, E.J.   Marshall, TX   President of Texas & Gulf Railroad; Owner Fry-Hodge Drug Co.; Grand Commander of San Antonio Knights of Templar.

Gaines, R.R.   Austin, TX   Texas Supreme Court Chief Justice.

Galbraith, R.M.   Pine Bluff, AR   Principal of Pine Bluff Power & Transit Co.

Garitty, James   Corsicana, TX   Director of Texas Petroleum Co.; Pres. of Texas Cotton Growers; President of First National Bank; Director of Cotton Belt Railroad; Committee member of intracoastal waterway project; Was "overcome by a gas well and died" in 1905.

Garrison, D.E.   St. Louis, MO   Principal of Columbia Incandescent Lamp Co.

Gaston, Wm. H.   Dallas, TX   Banker; Principal in Gaston & Ayre; Honorary title of Colonel; National Republican committeeman.

Gates, John W.   New York, NY   Director of Producer's Oil (Spindletop); Pioneer promoter of barbed wire; Director of Kansas City Southern Railway; President of Republic Steel and the Texas Co. (Texaco); Known as "Bet-a-Million Gates," the American Gilded Age industrialist and gambler.

George, J.M.   San Antonio, TX   San Antonio
postmaster; Partner in San Jose Land Co.; Director of Commercial
Exchange; Avid duck hunter, tarpon fisherman, and skeet shooter.
Gilmore, S.J.   Denver, CO   President of New
Loveland & Greeley Irrigation & Land Co.; President of Northern
Colorado Irrigation Co.
Glidden, C.J.   Lowell, MA   Director of Lowell
Land Co.; Owned one of the first "auto-cars" in Boston (1901);
Automobile racer and sponsor of C.J. Glidden Touring Trophy in 1905.
Glogau, Emile   St. Louis, MO   Died in 1900
Godley, R.B.   Dallas, TX   President of R.B.
Godley Lumber Co.; Director of Ninth National Bank of Dallas.
Gordon, Jack   Paris, TX   Principal in Moore,
Robinson & Adams Insurance Co.; Director of Bryan Driving Assoc.;
Founded a game and hunting preserve in Indian territory.
Gould, Edwin   New York, NY   Heir to Jay Gould
estate; Investor; Member of Jekyll Island Club, Georgia.
Graham, B.B.   St. Louis, MO   President of Graham
Paper Co.; Principal in St. Louis Union Trust Co.
Grant, J.B.   Denver, CO   Governor; Principal
Omaha & Grant Smelting Co.; Chairman of American Smelting &
Refining Co.
Grant, John   Paris, TX   US Eastern District
Marshall; National Republican committeeman for Texas.
Gratz, Benjamin   St. Louis, MO   Principal of Warren,
Jones & Gratz Manufacturing; Famously established a monopoly on
neckties in 1896.
Graves, Amos   San Antonio, TX   Physician
Green, E.H.R.   Terrell, TX   Director of Texas
Midland Railroad.
Green, G.H.   Dallas, TX   Businessman; Cotton
investments; Active Shriner.
Grice, Frank   San Antonio, TX   Publisher of *San
Antonio Express.*
Grigsby, G.M.D.   Jefferson, TX   President of Texas &
Sabine Railway; President of Texas & Gulf Railroad.
Grinnan, J.S.   Terrell, TX   Principal of J.S.
Grinnan Seed Farm Co.; Manager North Texas Insane Asylum; Title of
Major.

Haarstick, Wm. T.   St. Louis, MO   Capitalist; President
of Merchants Exchange, Sporting excursions throughout the south for
ducks and deer.

222

Hall, W.L.	Dallas, TX	Attorney for Texas &

Pacific Railway Co.

Hall, Kirk	Dallas, TX	Dallas Alderman;

Involved in Democratic party politics.

Hallett, M.	Denver CO	Judge
Hamilton, Charles H.	Waco, TX	Vice President of

Texas & Pacific Railway; Honorary title of Colonel.

Hamilton, Henry	Dallas, TX	Finance; Dallas

Alderman; 1898 member and on the Board of Directors; Involved in
Republican politics

Hamilton, H.E.	Dallas, TX	Banker
Hammond, F.M.	Lancaster, TX	Principal of F.H.

Hammond & Co. and Lancaster Gin Co.

Hampton, J.W.	Abilene, TX	Principal of Lowden

National Bank.

Handlan, A.H.	St. Louis, MO	President of Buck

Railway Supply Co.; Director of M.M. Buck Manufacturing Co.

Hardwick, W.P.	Fort Worth, TX	President of Worth

Hotel Co.

Hare, Silas, Jr.	Sherman, TX	Attorney; Judge;

Banker.

Harrington, C.E.	Denver, CO	No information
Harris, John	Terrell, TX	No information
Harrison, W.B.	Fort Worth, TX	President of State

National Bank; Treasurer of City of Ft. Worth; Director of Glover-
Anderson Oil Co.

Harry, D.W.C.	Dallas, TX	Vice President of

National Bank of Commerce.

Harry, T.C.	Dallas, TX	Director of Dallas

Cable Railway Co., and Dallas Commercial Club; Active in Democratic
party politics.

Hart, E.A.	Cincinnati, OH	Attorney
Haynes, J.J.	Laredo, TX	Collector of

Customs; President of Texas Bermuda Onion Association.; 1908
Republican Convention delegate; Co-owner of Laredo Baseball Assoc.

Heard, Bryan	Houston, TX	President of

McFadden Bros. Cotton Agency; Principal in Bryan Heard Oil Co.; Board
of Directors of Texas Bank and Trust; President of Texas State
Sportsmen's Association; Commodore Houston Launch Club; Golfing
champion.

Heath, P.S.	Washington, DC	Correspondent for

Indianapolis Journal; US Postmaster General; Principal in P.S. Heath &
Co.; Secretary of the Republican National Committee; Honorary title of
Colonel.

Heflry, W.T. Cameron, TX Real estate; 1894
Democratic Convention delegate.
Higgins, C.C. Bastrop, TX Physician
Hodgman, C. St. Louis, MO Principal in White &
Hodgman.
Hogg, James S. Austin, TX Attorney; Texas
Governor 1891 - 1895; Created Texas Railroad Commission.
Holland, Frank Dallas, TX Dallas Mayor;
Newspaper editor; Publisher of *Holland's Magazine* and *Farm & Ranch*
(magazine); Member of Dallas Commercial Club; Founded the Oaks Shore
Hunting Preserve in Fulton in 1905.
Hollins, H.B. New York, NY President of H.B.
Hollins & Co.; Invested in and directed railroads and banks.
Hopkins, James St. Louis, MO President of
Producer's Oil (Spindletop Field); Director of Kansas City Southern
Railway.
Hornby, John Fort Worth, TX County Judge; 1902
Democratic candidate for railroad commissioner.
House, T.W. Houston, TX Director of Texas
Midland Railroad; President of T.W. House Bank; Treasurer for Gen. Sam
Houston monument fund-raising effort.
Houston, A.W. San Antonio, TX Judge; Texas
Senator; Democrat; Fished for tarpon at Aransas Pass as early as 1896;
1898 and 1899 Tarpon Club Board of Directors; Committee for San
Antonio International Fair; Honorary member of 1907 Port Aransas
Tarpon Club.
Houston, Reagan San Antonio, TX Attorney for San
Antonio & Aransas Pass Railway.
Hoxie, G.H. Chicago, IL Cattleman and owner
of Thorn Creek Herefords.
Hughes, C.J. Denver, CO Attorney; 1904
candidate for Colorado governor.
Hughes, W.E. Dallas, TX President of Windsor
and Tremont hotels in Galveston; Honorary Colonel; Cattleman.
Hugo, Charles San Antonio, TX President of Alamo
National Bank.
Hunter, R.D. Fort Worth, TX Principal in Hunter-
Phelan Savings and Trust Co.; Director of Spindletop Oil Co.; President of
Thurber Mining Co.; President of Texas and Pacific Coal Co.; Honorary
Colonel.
Huntington, C.P. New York, NY Industrialist;
Railroad investor; Central Pacific Railroad; Southern Pacific Railroad;
Died in 1900; Hetty Green nemesis because of his financial manipulations.

James, Harry C.   Denver, CO   Director of Holly
Sugar Co. & Portland Cement Co.
Johnson, Jefferson R.   Austin, TX   Commissioner of
Agriculture, Insurance, Statistics & History.
Jones, B.   St. Louis, MO   No information
Jones, Jesse H.   Houston, TX   Principal in South
Texas Lumber Co.; Banker; Real Estate.

Kampmann, H. D.   San Antonio, TX   Real estate investor;
Manager of Menger Hotel. NOTE: Original 1899 club membership book
spelling was KAMPMAN.
Keating, C.A.   Dallas, TX   Director of Dallas
Terminal Railroad & Union Depot Co.
Kenedy, John G.   Alice, TX   Ranching; Investor
in St. Louis, Brownsville & Mexico Railroad; Heir to Mifflin Kenedy,
operated the Kenedy Ranch; Also had home and office in Corpus Christi,
Texas.
Kenna, E.D.   Chicago, IL   Vice President of
Saint Paul Railroad; Married daughter of club member R. C. Kerens.
Kerens, R.C.   St. Louis, MO   President of National
Bank of Kansas City; Politician; Ambassador to Vienna; Candidate for US
Senate; Head of National and Missouri Republican National Committee.
Kleberg, Robert J.   Corpus Christi, TX   Lawyer; Managed
King Ranch for his mother-in-law, Henrietta King.
Knight, H.F.   St. Louis, MO   Investor; Vice
President of A. G. Edwards & Sons Brokerage Co.
Koehler, Otto   San Antonio, TX   President of City
Brewery; President of Texas Rubber Co.; Committee for San Antonio
International Fair.
Kokernot, J.W.   San Antonio, TX   Ranching and cattle;
President of San Antonio International Fair; Active in local politics.
Kountze, C.B.   Denver, CO   Capitalist

Lasater, Ed C.   San Antonio, TX   Ranching, Cattle;
Nominated for 1902 Republican state senator.
Lee, W.H.   San Antonio, TX   President of
Merchants-Laclede National Bank; Director of Union Trust Co. of
St. Louis.
Leith, J.E.   Terrell, TX   Agent for Texas
Midland Railroad.
Leman, L.E.   Denver, CO   No information
Lewis, H.C.   St. Louis, MO   Attorney
Lewis, Perry J.   San Antonio, TX   Democratic state
senator; Fished tarpon at Aransas Pass as early as 1896.

Lindsay, J.M.   Gainesville, TX   Judge; President of Gainesville, McAlester & St. Louis Railway; Director of Gainesville, Oklahoma & Gulf Railway.

Lindsay, L.B.   Gainesville, TX   Principal in National Telephone Construction Co. of Texas.

Lionberger, Isaac H.   St. Louis, MO   Real estate

Lockwood, J.S.   San Antonio, TX   Director of Texas Midland Railroad; President of Lockwood National Bank; 1898 Tarpon Club Board of Directors; Was the first person in Texas to catch a tarpon over 100 pounds on rod and reel.

Lowry, R.J.   Atlanta, GA   President of Lowry National Bank; Honorary title of Colonel.

Loyd, M.B.   Fort Worth, TX   Director of Texas Midland Railroad; President of Fort Worth Union Depot; President of Texas Bankers Assoc.; Organized drill team M. B. Rifles of Fort Worth.

Lucas, John B.C.   St. Louis, MO   Capitalist; Director of American Exchange Bank; Vice President of St. Charles Bridge Co.; Author R.K. Sawyer's great-great grandfather.

Lyon, Cecil A.   Sherman, TX   President of Lyon-Gray Lumber Co.; Vice President of Hardeman Co. Irrigation Co.; Director of Great Southern Life Insurance Co.; 1902 Chairman State Republican Executive Committee.

McCampbell, E. Atlee   Corpus Christi, TX   Attorney; Real estate investor; Died in 1902.

McDonald, B.P.   Waco, TX   Director of Missouri, Kansas & Texas Railroad.

McElhone, F.H.   Dallas, TX   Agent for Fireman's Fund Insurance Co.

McEntire, W.R.   Dallas, TX   Ranching and cattle

McGown, Floyd   San Antonio   Attorney; Principal San Antonio Police and Fire Commission; Active in San Antonio politics.

McGrath, Wm. H.   Dallas, TX   Mechanical engineer; Principal of Dallas Waterworks; Principal of Dallas Steam Candy Co.; Principal of General Fire Extinguisher Co. of Texas.

McHenry, Estell   St. Louis, MO   Member of 1904 St. Louis World's Fair Committee.

McLemore, Jefferson A.   Austin, TX   Publisher/Editor of *Corpus Christi Herald* and *Gulf Coast Magazine*; Democrat state senator

McLendon, J.S.   Waco, TX   President of Waco First National Bank; Treasurer for Waco, Hamilton & Brownwood Railroad Co.

McMillan, W.N.   St. Louis, MO   Heir to American Car & Foundry Co.; Presented lions and leopards to San Antonio Zoo.

McNaught, F.H.	Denver	Surgeon
Madill, G.A.	St. Louis, MO	Judge; Director of

Sedalia Electric Light & Power Co.

Mallam, G.H.	Beaumont, TX	Principal in Texas

Tram and Lumber Co.; Principal in Village Mills Co.

Mallinckrodt, Edw.	St. Louis, MO	Principal in St. Louis

Union Trust Co.; NOTE: Original club membership book name spelled incorrectly.

Marshall, F.E.	St. Louis, MO	Treasury State

Commission; Cashier of Continental National Bank.

Martin, E.J.	San Antonio, TX	SAAP Railway

General Freight and Passenger Agent.

Martin, W.B.	Terrell, TX	Superintendent of

Southern Pacific Co.

Mason, J.T.	Denver, CO	Investor in Texas

cattle.

Maxwell J.W.	Dallas, TX	Superintendent of

Missouri, Kansas & Texas Railway.

Meade, G.P.	Fort Worth, TX	Attorney; Land

investor; Active in national politics.

Merchant, G.W.	Dallas, TX	Ranching and cattle
Miller, D.	St. Paul, MN	Director of Great

Northern Steamship Co.

Miller, Jeff N.	Houston, TX	Vice President, of St.

Louis, Brownsville & Mexico Railroad; Later founded Point Isabel Tarpon and Fishing Club.

Milroy, A.D.	Brenham, TX	Businessman;

President of Brenham Commercial Club.

Mims, S.	Ft. Worth, TX	Principal in Texas &

Pacific Coal Co. and Texas Pacific Mercantile & Manufacturing Co.

Minor, B.B., Jr.	Brenham, TX	Cotton Broker;

Physician.

Monserrate, M.D.	San Antonio, TX	Vice President and

Manager of SAAP Railway; Honorary title of Colonel.

Morse, C.S.	Austin, TX	Clerk for Missouri

Pacific Railway.

Morton, J.W.	St. Louis, MO	Politician; Candidate

for Senator in 1890.

Moss, S.E.	Cleburne, TX	Banker; Director of

Glover-Anderson Oil Co.; Manager of Cleburne Jockey Club; Principal in Johnson Grass Exterminator Co., Honorary title of Colonel; President of 1896 Dallas County Exposition; Competitive trap and skeet shooter.

Munson, J.T.   Denison, TX   President of
Southern Railway Construction Co.; Director of Denison & Wichita Valley
Railway.
Munson, W.B.   Denison, TX   President of
Sherman, Shreveport & Southern Railway; Director of Denison & Wichita
Valley Railway.
Murray, O.G.   Baltimore, MD   Principal at
Baltimore & Ohio Railroad.

Neidringhaus, T.K.   St. Louis, MO   Owner of
Neidringhaus Factory; State Republican Committee Chairman; Chairman
of St. Louis Police Board.
Newby, W.G.   Ft. Worth, TX   President of
American National Bank of Ft. Worth; Director of Texas Pacific
Manufacturing Co.; Principal of Globe Oil; Principal of Allen Motor Co.
Newell, O.S.   San Antonio, TX   Superintendent at
Pullman Co.; 1904 Republican Convention delegate.
Nunn, W.G.   Ladonia, TX   President of Weldan
National Bank.

O'Brien, Wm.   Aspen, CO   Director of Bolles
Livestock Co.; Principal at N.A. Riedell Investment Co.; NOTE: Original
club membership book spelling was OBREIN.
O'Connor, J.C.   Dallas, TX   President of Dallas
City National Bank; Director of Dallas Opera house; Involved in 1898
state Republican primaries.
O' Neil, A.H.   Paris, TX   Nominated for
Senator 1908.
Ogden, C.W.   San Antonio, TX   Attorney; Judge;
General counsel to Texas Midland Railroad; 1898 Republic Convention
delegate. Member 1896 Republican Executive Committee.
Oliver, R.   Groesbeck, TX   President of
Groesbeck National Bank.
Oppenheimer, D.G.   Dallas, TX   Businessman;
Incorporated the Silver Lake Hunting & Fishing Club of Dallas.

Paramore, Fred W.   St. Louis, MO   Banker; President of
Paramore Investment Co.; Director of Mississippi Valley Trust Co.
Parker, John W.   Taylor, TX   Attorney for San
Antonio & Gulf Shore Railway.
Patterson, W.H.   New York, NY   Military General;
Owned insurance companies; Active in Texas Democratic politics;
Founder Koon Kreek Klub, Athens, Texas.

Peeler, J.L.   Austin, TX   Attorney; 1908
Democratic senatorial candidate; Honorary title of Colonel.
Perin, Clifford   Cincinnati, OH   Clothing
manufacturing; Principal at Bahlman, & Smith Co.; Member of National
Steeplechase Assn.; Owned an English coach drawn by four horses; Died
on his yacht in 1902.
Perin, F.L.   Cincinnati, OH   Director of Third
National Bank of Cincinnati; President of Millcreek Distilling Co.
Peters, T.E.   Colorado Springs, Co   Foreman of Central
City Register-Call.
Pierce, H. Clay   St. Louis, MO   Principal at Waters-
Pierce Oil Co.; Director of Kansas City Southern Railway; Involved in a
$5 million lawsuit with Standard Oil.
Pillot, Camille G.   Houston, TX   Owner of Henke
Pillot grocery stores; 1892 Harris Co. Democratic delegate; Vice President
of Texas State Sportsmen's Assoc. Member of Maner Lake Hunting &
Fishing Club and Eagle Lake Rod & Gun Club.
Polk, L.J.   Galveston, TX   Vice President of
Gulf, Colorado & Santa Fe Railway.
Poor, Henry W.   New York, NY   Banking; President
of H. W. Poor Co. with offices in Boston and Wall St., NY.
Potter, R.E.   Dallas, TX   Rancher
Priest, H.S.   St. Louis, MO   Attorney for
Missouri Pacific Railroad; US District Judge; 1902 candidate for senator;
President of Missouri State Bar Assn.

Quinlan, G.A.   Houston, TX   Vice President of
Houston & Texas Central Railroad.

Randolph, Tom   Sherman, TX   President of
Merchants & Planters National Bank; President of Commonwealth Trust
Co. of St. Louis; Vice President of National Bank of Commerce St. Louis.
Reardon, E.M.   Dallas, TX   President of Dallas
City National Bank; Treasurer of Dallas Terminal Railroad & Union Depot
Co.; Tarpon Club 1898 and 1899 Board of Directors and 1899 Secretary.
Reynolds, W.D.   Albany, TX   President of
Reynolds Land & Cattle Co.; Vice President of Albany First National
Bank; President of Stamford First National Bank.
Reynolds, G.T.   Albany, TX   Rancher; President
of Albany First National Bank; Chairman of Democratic Executive
Committee.
Reynolds, W.D.   Denver CO   Manager of Gulf,
Colorado & Santa Fe Railway; NOTE: Original 1899 club membership
book spelling was W.E.

229

Richardson, J.C. St. Louis, MO President of
Chemical National Bank.
Ridgeway, A.C. Florence, CO General
Superintendent of Florence & Cripple Creek Railway; General Manager of
Denver & Rio Grande Railway Co.
Ripley, Dan Galveston, TX Manager of Houston,
Texas Central & Southern Pacific Railway; Agent of Lone Star Steamship
Line.
Roberts, M.C. Terrell, TX Businessman
Robertson, J.H. Austin, TX Attorney
Robins, M.L. Houston, TX Agent for Houston &
Texas Central Railway.
Robinson, D.B. St. Louis, MO President of St.
Louis & San Francisco Railroad; Vice President of Atchison, Topeka &
Santa Fe Railroad.
Ross, T.D. Ft. Worth, TX Principal at Powell
Loan & Mortgage Co.; Manager, Western Security Co.
Rotan, Edward Waco, TX President of First
National Bank of Waco.
Rouse, H.C. New York, NY President of
Missouri, Kansas & Texas Railroad Co.; President of Boonville Railroad
Bridge Co.; Director at Denison & Wichita Valley Railway; Commodore
of Seawankaka Yacht Club.

Sanders, J.F. Denver, CO Director of Delta
Packing Co.; Mine owner; Director of Farmers & Merchants Bank.
Sanger, Alex P. Dallas, TX Vice Pres of Dallas
Terminal Railroad & Union Depot Co.
Sawyer, W.E. Lacrosse, WI Editor of *Horicon*
Reporter.
Schneider, Julius E. Dallas, TX Vice President of
Dallas City National Bank; Hosted Tarpon Club member Edwin Gould at
Texas State Fair in 1895.
Schofield, J.D. Dallas, TX Principal at J.D.
Schofield Manufacturing Co.; Patented a Shofield Disc Planter; Principal
in Dallas Auto Club.
Scott, H.C. St. Louis, MO Vice President of
Clinton Stoneware Co.
Seeger, J.B. Dallas, TX Businessman;
Principal of Woodworth Cycle Co.
Seley, Wm. W. Waco, TX President of Waco
State Bank; Director of First National Bank; Director of Cotton Palace.
Senn, Nicolas Chicago, IL Surgeon; President
of American Medical Association.

230

Simpson, John N.   Dallas, TX   Director of Missouri, Kansas & Texas Railroad; Cattleman and Rancher; 1898 club Board of Directors; Member Dallas Commercial Club; Honorary title of Colonel.

Skinner, G.W.   Denver, CO   Principal of Missouri, Kansas & Texas Railroad.

Smith, S.F.   Denver, CO   No information

Snider, A.J.   Kansas City, MO   Real Estate

Snyder, R.M.   Kansas City, MO   President of City National Bank; Convicted of bribery in 1903.

Soper, Arthur W.   New York, NY   President of Pintsch Compressing Co.

Speer, H. F.   Dallas, TX   Dallas City Alderman.

Spencer, J.W.   Ft. Worth, TX   President of Ft. Worth Farmers & Mechanics National Bank; Director; Fort Worth Chamber of Commerce; President Indian Relief Fund. NOTE: Original 1899 club membership book spelling was SPENSER.

Staacke, H.G.   San Antonio, TX   Principal at Staacke Bros. Wagons & Carriages; Director of San Antonio Automobile Club.

Stevens, John J.   San Antonio, TX   Principal of Texas Rubber Co.; San Antonio Postmaster.

Stevens, G.A.   Moline, IL   Vice President of Moline Plow Co.

Stewart, D.A.   Dallas, TX   Investor; Principal at Duff, Domanau & Bros.; Member of 1904 Democratic Executive Committee.

Stillman, T.E.   New York, NY   Director of Brooklyn Heights Railroad.

Sugg, E.C.   Indian Territory   Cattleman; Principal at E.C. Suggs & Bros.; Moved to Gainesville, Texas.

Sullivan, D.J.   San Antonio, TX   Attorney for D. Sullivan & Co.

Sullivan, W. C.   San Antonio, TX   Attorney for D. Sullivan & Co.; Active in Democratic politics.

Swenson, E.P.   New York, NY   Banker at S. M. Swenson & Sons, Wall St.; Developed paved roads in New York mountains for holiday travelers.

Swenson, S.A.   New York, NY   Banker at S. M. Swenson & Sons, Wall St.; His lodge in the New York mountains was leased by John D. Rockefeller.

Swope, Joseph   Dallas, TX   Principal at Swope & Mangold Mercantile of Dallas.

Terrell, Edwin H.   San Antonio, TX   Attorney; Vice President of San Antonio Gas Company and San Antonio Board of Trade; Minister to Belgium; 1880, 1888, and 1904 Republican National Convention delegate; Member of Republican state executive committee, 1894 -1900.

Thatcher, J.A.   Denver, CO   Banker

Thompson, C.A.   St. Louis, MO   No information

Thompson, Wm.   Dallas, TX   Attorney

Thompson, W.B.   St. Louis, MO   Attorney; Treasurer of 1900 Republican Congressional Committee.

Tips, Walter   Austin, TX   Vice President of Austin National Bank; Active in Democratic party politics.

Townsend, W.J.   Dallas, TX   Attorney; President of Angelina County National Bank.

Trezevant, T.J.   Dallas, TX   Director of Dallas Terminal Railroad & Union Depot Co.; Principal at Trezevant & Coke Insurance; NOTE: Original club membership book spelling was J.T.

Tullock, A.J.   Leavenworth, KS   President of Missouri Valley Bridge & Iron Works; Business associate of Andrew Carnegie.

Turner, W.G.   Ft. Worth, TX   President of Fort Worth Board of Trade.

Van Blarcom, J.C.   St. Louis, MO   Banker; President of National Bank of Commerce; 1898 club Board of Directors; Director of 1904 St. Louis World's Fair.

Wahrmund, Otto   San Antonio, TX   Vice President of San Antonio Brewing Assn.; President of Texas Transportation Co.; 1898 Republican senatorial candidate; President of San Antonio Fair Assn.

Walsh, E., Jr.   St. Louis, MO   Manufacturer with patents for a glass cutter, glass rolling machine, imitation leaded glass.

Ward, R.H.   Ft. Worth, TX   Judge; Assistant Attorney General; Politician; Involved in Democratic politics.

Warner, S.G.   Tyler, TX   Agent for St. Louis Southwestern Railway; Agent for Kansas City, Pittsburg & Gulf Railroad.

Webb, Sam   Albany, TX   Attorney; President of Webb & Hill Real Estate; President of Albany First National Bank.

Wells, James   Dallas, TX   Contractor; Confederate Civil War veteran; 1890 Democratic Convention delegate, (Not to be confused with Brownsville Judge James B. Wells, who was solicited for membership in 1898.)

Wells, Rolla   St. Louis, MO   St. Louis Mayor

Welton, L.M.   San Antonio, TX   President of L.M. Welton & Co.; President of San Antonio Baseball Assn.

232

Wentz, D.B.	St. Louis, MO	President of National

Coal Assn.; Honorary title of Colonel.

West, T.F.	Ft. Worth, TX	Attorney for St.

Louis & San Francisco Railroad; Judge; Principal in American Dry Goods
Co. of Cleburne.

Whitney, Alfred R.	New York, NY	Stockbroker for A.

R. Whitney, Jr. & Co.; Trophied tarpon fisherman who wintered in Florida.

Whitaker, Edward	St. Louis, MO	President of St.

Louis Transit Co.

Whiteselle, J.E.	Corsicana, TX	Vice President of

First National Bank of Corsicana; Director of Austin Fire Insurance Co.;
Vice President of Texas Light Harness Horse Assn.

Wickes, T.H.	Chicago, IL	Vice President of

Pullman Co.

Williams, G.H.	Paris, TX	Agent for Gulf,

Colorado & Santa Fe Railway; Invested in racehorses.

Wilmot, E.P.	Austin, TX	President of Austin

National Bank.

Winchell, B.L.	Denver, CO	Vice President of

Colorado & Southern Railroad Co.

Wolf, H.O.	Dallas, TX	Investor
Wood, S.N.	Denver, CO	Director of Colorado

Short Line Co.

Wood, H.E.	Denver, CO	Capitalist at Wood

Investment Co.

Woodward, W.H.	St. Louis, MO	President of

Woodward & Tierman Printing Co.

Wortham, L.J.	Austin, TX	Principal of *Star-*

Telegram; Congressman; Honorary title of Colonel; Manager of World's
Fair Commission of Texas.

Wright, Geo. M.	St. Louis, MO	Attorney; Judge

Yoakum, B.F.	St. Louis, MO	President of St.

Louis & San Francisco Railroad Co.; President of St. Louis, Brownsville &
Mexico Railroad; Principal in St. Louis Union Trust Co.

Zang, J.F.	Dallas, TX	President of Zang

Manufacturing Co.; President of Dallas Commercial Club.

The only known 1899 member who was either mistakenly left
off the 1899 roster or was added after the membership book was
published:

Jenkins, E.H.	San Antonio, TX	General Manager of

San Antonio Street Railway Co.

The persons below may have been members at the Tarpon Club between 1900 and 1903. Their participation at the Club is documented, but it is unclear if they were members or guests:

Armstrong, John   Dallas, TX   Physician: Active in
Republican politics.
Burdick, J.W.   Albany, NY   Manager of
Delaware & Hudson Railroad; Member of famous Southern Pacific 1905
hunting expedition in Mexico.
Carter, G.A.   Dallas, TX   Agent for Missouri,
Kansas & Texas Railroad; Active in Democratic politics.
Corcoran, Tommie   New Haven, CT   Shortstop, Cincinnati
Reds; Referenced only as an honorary Tarpon Club member.
Fargo, C.H.   Chicago, IL   Probably owner of
Fargo & Co. shoe manufacturing.
McDaniel, B.   Fort Scott, KS   Not available
Miller, J.G.   Saint Louis, MO   Attorney
Morrill, Edmund. N. Topeka, KS   Banking; Republican
governor of Kansas 1895 - 1897; Military Major.
Skinker, Thomas K. Saint Louis, MO   Judge

Newspapers reported that a number of prominent men, none of whose names were listed in the 1899 Tarpon Club Membership Book, were founding members of the Tarpon Club. It is likely that E.H.R. Green leaked their names for publicity:

Cleveland, Grover   Caldwell, NJ   US President from
1885-1889.
Culberson, Charles A. Jefferson, TX   Texas governor in
1890; US senator; Democrat.
Hanna, Mark A.   New Lisbon, OH   Ohio senator;
Chairman Republican National Committee; Traveled to Rockport in 1897
with Green but was the only one in the party who did not fish for tarpon.
McKinley, William   Niles, OH   US President from
1897-1901. Assassinated by Leon Czolgosz in 1901.
Quay, Matt S.   Dillsburg, PA   Pennsylvania
senator; Chairman Republican National Committee.
Sayers, Joseph D.   Bastrop, TX   Texas governor from
1898-1900; Democrat.

234

APPENDIX 3

SPORT, TEXAS RESIDENTS

The 1900 census page for Sport Texas is shown above. The first of the twenty-seven entries is that of E.H.R. Green, with an occupation of railroad president. Four families were living in the town: those of electrician Louis F. Bailey; 40-year-old hotel keeper A. R. A. 'Robert' Brice, 36-year-old sailor Andrew Sorenson, and servant Laura Griffen. Seven others were listed as servants, both male and female, hailing from Texas, Mexico, and Virginia. Mabel Harlow is not listed among the citizens of Sport, Texas.

SPORT, TEXAS RESIDENTS

Name	Occupation, etc.
Green, Edward E.H.	Rail Road President
Evans, Carl S.A.	Hotel Clerk
Bailey, Louis F.	Electrician
" Lizzie E.	Wife
" Louis F, Jr.	Son
" Marguerite	Daughter
Terry, John B.	Nephew
McCarthy, Stephen	Servant
Brice, Robert	Hotel Keeper
" Laura G.	Wife
" Robert H.	Son
" Bryson C.	Son
Hamilton, John	Servant
Sutton, Lizzie E.	Servant
Perez, Desmin	Servant
Hicks, Lexana	Servant
McCarthy, Puieley	Servant
Sigurez, Jack	Servant
Sorenson, Andrew	Sailor
" Sarah	Wife
" John H.	Son, high school
" Robert S.	Son
Griffin, Laura G.	Servant
" Jessie	Daughter
" James	Son
" Miss Janice	Daughter
" Brunett	Daughter

INDEX

Baldwin, B.B. Jr. 202, 216
Barnhart, G.W.   202, 216
Bass, Perry 129
Beddoe, T.D. 202, 216
Eebe Hotel 80
Beilharz, Theodore 202, 216
Bell, Thad C. 77, 202, 216
Bell, J.H. 77, 202, 217
Bellows Falls, Vermont 18, 19
Belo, A.H. 202, 217
Bergstrom, Oscar 202, 217
Bering, C.L. 81
Bewley, M.P. 202, 217
B. F. Meek & Sons 47
Bide a Wee Home (charity) 142
Big Fair and Auto Carnival 135
Bissell, J.B. 202, 217
Black, H.C. 202, 217
Black and Tans (political faction) 28, 30, 131, 132
Blackford, G.L. 202, 217
Blake, J.W. 203, 217
Blossom, H.A. 203, 217
Bludworth, Bernard Leonard 89, 114, 117
Bludworth, George James "Jim" 89, 114, 116, 117
Bludworth, John Leonard 88, 89, 114, 116, 117
Bludworth, Thomas "Jed" 88, 89, 116
Bolles, R.J. 203, 217   .
Bonner, WA. 203, 217
Booth, C.H. 102, 203, 217
Boren, B.N. 203, 217
Boyce, W.D. 76, 203, 217
Brackenridge, George W. 29, 77, 92, 203, 217
Brenizer, N.O. 203, 217
Brice, A.R.A. Robert 65, 123-126, 237
Brice, Laura G. 237
Brice, Robert H. 237
Brice, Bryson C. 237
Brown, J.G. 203, 217
Browning, John M. 36, 43, 44
Brujen, Mateo 107
Bryan, William Jennings 81
Bryant, W.G. 217
Bryant, W.H. 203, 217
Bryant, W.J. 33

239

Gould, Edwin 76, 206, 222
Gould, Jay 76
Graham, B.B. 206, 222
Grand Windsor Hotel 27
Grant, J.B. 77, 206, 222
Grant, John 206, 222
Gratz, Benjamin 206, 222
Graves, Amos 206, 222
Gray, Capt. Sam 50, 58
Gray Wolf (Automobile) 135
Green, E.H.R. see Green, Edward Howland Robinson
Green, Edward Henry 12, Marriage 15, Investments 15
Green, Edward Howland Robinson Childhood 18, 23, Mabel Harlow 24, 27, Marriage 140-41, Death 148, In Terrell Texas 24, 25, Texas Midland Railroad 24, 26, Tarpon Club 5, 49-57, Members 75-7, 206, 222, Closing 122, Politics 27-8, 121-24, 131-133, Yacht *Mabel* 53-4, *SS United States* 141-43, Lifesaving Station 64, Weather Room 64, Post Office 65, Hunting 95, Fishing 102-3, Hurricane 103, Yachting 113, 115-6, Inventions 133, Automobiles 133-6, Boll Weevil 136-7, Floral Company 137, Baseball 137, Airplanes 138, Ned (name)140, E.H.R. (name) 140, Colonel (honorary title) 139-40, Stamps and Coins 140, Round Hill 143, Mansion 144, Broadcasting Studio 144, WMAF Radio Station 144-5, *Charles W. Morgan* Whaling Ship 145, 150, Airport 145, Miami 147, Death 148, Estate 149-8
Green Floral Company 137
Green, G.H. 206, 222
Green, Hetty 13, 139, Wills (Inheritance) 14, Marriage 15, Mannerisms 15,16, 17, Railroad(s) 17, 18, Death 140, Estate 143
Grice, Frank 206, 222
Griffin, Laura 65, 237
Griffin, Jessie 237
Griffin, James 237
Griffin, Janice 237
Griffin, Brunett 236
Grigsby Construction Company 52
Grigsby, G.M.D. 206, 222
Grinnan, J.S. 206, 222
Guessaz, Oscar 92
Gulf Fisheries Company 128

Haarstick, Wm. T. 206, 222
Hall, W.L. 206, 223
Hall, Kirk 206, 223
Hallett, M. 206, 223

BOOKS BY R.K. SAWYER

A Hundred Years of Texas Waterfowl Hunting:
The Decoys, Guides, Clubs, and Places, 1870s to 1970s

Texas Market Hunting:
Stories of Waterfowl, Game Laws, and Outlaws

Images of the Hunt:
A Photographic History of Texas

Copies are available from
https://robertksawyer.com

BOOKS AVAILABLE
FROM
NUECES PRESS

1919 – The Storm
Corpus Christi – A History
A Soldier's Life
Great Tales from the History of South Texas
Recollections of Other Days
Perilous Trails of Texas
Columns   2009 – 2011
Columns 2 2012 – 2013
Columns 3 2014 – 2015
Columns 4 2016 – 2018
Streets of Corpus Christi Texas
Thomas Noakes Diary of War & Drought
100 Tales of Old Texas
Water Woes
Zachary Taylor's Army in Texas

*Copies and more information
are available at*
www.nuecespress.com